GRE Tunneling: Building Secure and Scalable VPNs

James Relington

DEDICATION

To those who seek knowledge, inspiration, and new perspectives—
may this book be a companion on your journey, a spark for curiosity,
and a reminder that every page turned is a step toward discovery.

AKNOWLEDGEMENTS

I would like to express my deepest gratitude to everyone who contributed to the creation of this book. To my colleagues and mentors, your insights and expertise have been invaluable. A special thank you to my family and friends for their unwavering support and encouragement throughout this journey.

Introduction to GRE Tunneling

Generic Routing Encapsulation, commonly known as GRE, is a tunneling protocol designed to encapsulate a wide variety of network layer protocols into point-to-point connections. Initially developed by Cisco Systems, GRE has become a fundamental component in modern networking, especially in the context of Virtual Private Networks (VPNs), where it serves as a lightweight and flexible solution to interconnect distant networks across an untrusted medium such as the internet. The primary utility of GRE lies in its ability to transport packets from one protocol over another protocol, making it an ideal mechanism for protocol-independent encapsulation. This encapsulation capability makes GRE highly suitable for situations where legacy protocols or non-IP traffic need to traverse IP-based infrastructures.

The basic concept behind GRE tunneling involves the creation of a virtual point-to-point link between two endpoints, known as tunnel interfaces. Once established, this virtual link allows the encapsulation of entire packets within another IP header, effectively enabling the transmission of data between geographically dispersed networks. What makes GRE particularly valuable is its simplicity and protocol-agnostic nature. Unlike more complex tunneling mechanisms that are often bound to specific encryption or security standards, GRE focuses solely on encapsulation, leaving encryption and integrity to be handled by complementary technologies such as IPsec when necessary. This modular approach provides network architects with a high degree of flexibility in designing VPN architectures that are both secure and scalable.

One of the key characteristics of GRE is that it supports the encapsulation of multicast and broadcast traffic, a feature that differentiates it from simpler IP-in-IP tunneling techniques. This capability is especially important when running dynamic routing protocols such as OSPF, EIGRP, or RIP over the tunnel, as these protocols rely on multicast to communicate with peers. By enabling this type of traffic to traverse the tunnel, GRE ensures that routing updates and advertisements can function as if the networks were directly connected, which greatly simplifies the overall routing configuration and enhances convergence.

From a technical standpoint, GRE operates by wrapping an original packet, known as the payload, with a new GRE header and an outer IP header. The GRE header contains fields that identify the encapsulated protocol, provide optional checksum or key information, and indicate other control bits relevant to the tunnel's behavior. The outer IP header contains the source and destination IP addresses of the tunnel endpoints, effectively routing the encapsulated packet across the intermediate network. Upon reaching the destination, the GRE header is removed and the original packet is forwarded based on its own addressing information. This seamless encapsulation and decapsulation process is transparent to both the source and the destination of the payload traffic, which allows GRE to act as an invisible conduit between the two.

In practice, configuring a GRE tunnel requires defining tunnel interfaces on both ends of the connection and assigning them IP addresses from the same subnet. The tunnel source and destination must be specified using reachable IP addresses, typically public IPs or private IPs that can be routed via intermediary paths. Once the tunnel is established, it behaves like a virtual link, and routing protocols can be configured to send traffic through it just as they would on a physical interface. This ability to abstract away the underlying physical path and present a consistent logical connection is a powerful tool for network engineers who need to maintain connectivity across disparate infrastructure segments.

Despite its many advantages, GRE is not without limitations. The protocol itself does not provide confidentiality, authentication, or integrity. This means that GRE tunnels are susceptible to packet sniffing and spoofing unless paired with a security mechanism such as IPsec. While this separation of concerns allows GRE to remain lightweight and efficient, it also places the burden of securing the traffic on the network designer. Additionally, because GRE adds an extra header to each packet, it increases the overall packet size, which can lead to fragmentation issues if the resulting packet exceeds the maximum transmission unit (MTU) of the path. These challenges must be carefully managed through techniques such as path MTU discovery and appropriate security policies.

GRE has found widespread adoption in a variety of use cases, from simple site-to-site tunnels connecting branch offices to more complex scenarios such as tunneling traffic through firewalls, supporting mobile IP applications, and enabling cross-cloud or hybrid cloud connectivity. Its flexibility has also made it a go-to solution for carriers and service providers who need to offer Layer 3 VPN services over shared infrastructure. In modern networks, GRE is often deployed alongside other tunneling protocols such as IPsec, L2TP, or VXLAN, each serving different purposes within a layered and resilient architecture.

As networking continues to evolve toward more dynamic and software-defined models, GRE remains relevant due to its simplicity and reliability. While it may not provide the advanced features of newer tunneling protocols, its fundamental role as an encapsulation mechanism ensures that it continues to be an essential tool in the networking toolkit. Its ability to carry diverse types of traffic, maintain compatibility with routing protocols, and integrate with security layers makes it a foundational component for building scalable and secure virtual private networks in both traditional and modern environments.

Understanding GRE tunneling is a crucial first step for any network engineer looking to build or maintain complex internetworks. Its deployment is straightforward, its behavior is predictable, and its integration with other technologies is seamless when properly configured. By mastering the principles and operations of GRE, professionals can leverage its strengths to create robust and adaptable VPN solutions that meet the demands of modern connectivity.

History and Evolution of GRE

The development of Generic Routing Encapsulation, or GRE, is closely tied to the evolution of internetworking during the early days of the Internet. As networks began to expand across different technologies, hardware platforms, and protocol stacks, the need for a mechanism that could bridge these diverse environments became apparent. During the 1980s and 1990s, network engineers faced the challenge of connecting dissimilar networks using various protocols like IPX, AppleTalk, and DECnet, all of which needed to traverse an increasingly IP-dominated infrastructure. Cisco Systems responded to this need by introducing GRE as a versatile solution for encapsulating and transporting a wide range of network layer protocols over IP. At the time, there were limited options available for such encapsulation, and GRE quickly distinguished itself by offering a lightweight, protocol-agnostic framework that could easily be implemented and extended.

Initially, GRE was designed as a proprietary tunneling protocol to facilitate the encapsulation of any Layer 3 protocol within another Layer 3 protocol. This made it possible for organizations to migrate toward IP-based networks while continuing to support legacy systems and protocols. The first implementations of GRE allowed engineers to establish virtual point-to-point links between routers over an IP network, essentially simulating a direct physical connection. This was a powerful concept, as it meant that remote networks could be integrated into a unified topology regardless of the underlying infrastructure. GRE soon became popular in enterprise and service provider environments alike, especially for enabling interoperability and for simplifying routing in complex network designs.

Recognizing its usefulness, the Internet Engineering Task Force (IETF) formalized GRE as a standard in the mid-1990s. The first major specification was documented in RFC 1701, published in 1994. This RFC laid out the basic GRE header structure and encapsulation methods, providing a standardized approach to its implementation. Shortly thereafter, RFC 1702 followed, detailing how GRE could be used to tunnel IP packets specifically. These documents provided a solid foundation for GRE's deployment across a broad range of networking equipment and established it as a reliable tool for building virtual tunnels over IP networks.

However, as GRE saw wider use, engineers began to recognize certain limitations in the original specification, especially around security, simplicity, and compatibility. To address these concerns, RFC 2784 was published in 2000, superseding the earlier specifications and simplifying the GRE header by focusing solely on the encapsulation of IP packets. This version eliminated optional fields that had proven unnecessary or underutilized, making GRE lighter and easier to implement in both hardware and software. Around the same time, enhancements to GRE were introduced through additional RFCs such as RFC 2890, which added support for optional key and sequence number fields. These enhancements improved the protocol's flexibility and made it suitable for more advanced applications, including those requiring tunnel identification or basic replay protection.

Throughout the 2000s, GRE became a cornerstone of many enterprise and service provider VPN solutions. Its lightweight nature and ability to encapsulate multicast and broadcast traffic made it an ideal partner for dynamic routing protocols like OSPF and EIGRP, which rely on such traffic to maintain neighbor relationships and exchange routing information. This capability distinguished GRE from other encapsulation mechanisms like IP-in-IP, which could only handle unicast traffic. As organizations increasingly needed to support dynamic routing over virtual links, GRE became a default choice in many designs.

At the same time, GRE began to be used in conjunction with other technologies, particularly IPsec. While GRE itself did not provide encryption or authentication, it could be combined with IPsec to secure the encapsulated traffic. This layered approach gave network architects the best of both worlds: the flexibility of GRE for routing and protocol support, and the strong security guarantees of IPsec for confidentiality and integrity. This combination became especially popular in scenarios involving branch office connectivity, multi-site networks, and secure extranet connections.

As networking moved further into the era of virtualization and cloud computing, GRE adapted to the new requirements. Vendors began implementing GRE support in virtualized routers, cloud appliances, and software-defined networking (SDN) controllers. This allowed organizations to extend their networks across cloud platforms, support virtual workloads, and interconnect data centers with a consistent and efficient tunneling mechanism. GRE's minimal overhead made it especially attractive for high-throughput scenarios, where performance was critical. Its stateless operation and simplicity continued to make it easier to troubleshoot and deploy than more complex tunneling alternatives.

The rise of multiprotocol support and increased virtualization also led to the development of variants and derivatives of GRE, such as NVGRE (Network Virtualization using GRE). NVGRE was proposed as a solution for virtualized data centers, enabling isolation of tenant traffic in multi-tenant environments. While NVGRE never achieved the same level of adoption as its cousin VXLAN, it reflected the ongoing evolution of GRE into new domains and use cases. GRE's adaptability and extensibility proved once again to be among its greatest strengths.

Today, GRE remains a foundational protocol in many networking environments. Its relevance persists not because it is the most modern or feature-rich protocol, but because it does exactly what it was designed to do with remarkable efficiency and reliability. From its early days bridging incompatible networks to its modern role supporting cloud integration, GRE has continually proven its value as a simple, effective, and dependable tunneling protocol. Its evolution over time has been marked by pragmatic improvements and real-world testing, making it one of the most trusted tools in the network engineer's arsenal. As network infrastructure continues to evolve, GRE is likely to remain a key component of the tunneling landscape, appreciated for its clarity of purpose and its enduring flexibility.

GRE in the OSI Model

Understanding where GRE fits within the OSI model is crucial for network engineers and architects who aim to design, troubleshoot, and optimize complex network topologies. The OSI model, or Open Systems Interconnection model, is a conceptual framework used to understand and standardize the functions of a telecommunication or networking system. It divides networking into seven layers, from the physical transmission of bits at Layer 1 to the final user application at Layer 7. GRE, or Generic Routing Encapsulation, is a tunneling protocol that operates within this layered framework by facilitating the encapsulation of entire packets, including their headers, for transport across different parts of a network. While GRE itself is not explicitly bound to a single layer, its behavior and interaction with other network components allow it to be most accurately placed at Layer 3, the Network Layer.

GRE operates by encapsulating packets from a variety of network layer protocols inside IP packets, effectively allowing the transport of those protocols over an IP-based network. In the context of the OSI model, this places GRE as a function that occurs above Layer 2 and firmly within Layer 3. At this layer, GRE provides a mechanism for encapsulating Layer 3 payloads, such as IPv4, IPv6, or even other encapsulated protocols, into a new IP packet with its own outer header. This encapsulated packet can then be routed through the IP network to its destination, where the outer header and GRE wrapper are removed, and the original packet is forwarded to its final destination. By performing this function, GRE acts as a Network Layer protocol that supports the virtual extension of network boundaries.

GRE's role at Layer 3 makes it a powerful tool for interconnecting networks that are not directly connected. Since routing decisions are made at this layer, GRE tunnels are treated like any other routed IP interface. The encapsulated traffic appears to traverse a direct connection, even though it is moving through an underlying IP network that could span multiple physical links and administrative domains. Because the GRE tunnel endpoint assigns IP addresses to the virtual tunnel interfaces, these interfaces can participate in standard IP routing just like physical interfaces. This abstraction is central to many

VPN architectures, where the illusion of a direct connection is essential for proper routing behavior.

Despite operating at Layer 3, GRE has implications for other layers as well. For example, the data being encapsulated within a GRE tunnel can originate from higher-layer protocols such as TCP or UDP, which reside at Layer 4, the Transport Layer. This means that GRE must be capable of preserving the integrity and structure of these upper-layer payloads as they are transported across the network. Similarly, GRE relies on the services of the underlying IP infrastructure, which ultimately depends on the functionality of the Data Link Layer (Layer 2) and the Physical Layer (Layer 1) for actual transmission. Therefore, while GRE is a Layer 3 protocol, it interacts with and influences multiple layers of the OSI model.

One of the unique characteristics of GRE is that it can encapsulate packets multiple times, resulting in what is sometimes referred to as recursive encapsulation. In these scenarios, an already encapsulated GRE packet can be re-encapsulated within another GRE tunnel or another tunneling protocol altogether. This kind of multi-layer encapsulation can blur the boundaries of the OSI model, as multiple instances of Layer 3 processing occur within a single end-to-end communication. This recursive encapsulation is sometimes used in advanced network designs, such as provider backbone transport or complex overlay networks, to provide additional segmentation or control.

While GRE is agnostic to the payload it carries, it still requires a reliable transport mechanism at the IP level. The outer IP header added by GRE must be routable through the underlying network, which means that the GRE tunnel endpoints must have reachable IP addresses. This routing requirement firmly anchors GRE's operation to the Network Layer, where it depends on underlying routing protocols and infrastructure to deliver encapsulated packets. Unlike application-level tunneling protocols, which may rely on user-space operations and socket-level communication, GRE operates at a level that is intimately tied to the core routing logic of the system. Its implementation typically resides in the kernel of network devices or operating systems, ensuring efficient processing of encapsulated packets.

In terms of OSI model interaction, GRE also has implications for the Transport Layer. While it does not itself provide transport layer functions like port numbering, segmentation, or flow control, the transport layer protocols encapsulated within GRE must remain functional and compatible with the tunneling process. GRE introduces overhead in the form of additional headers, which can impact the Maximum Transmission Unit (MTU) and lead to fragmentation. This can be problematic for transport protocols such as TCP, which rely on accurate MTU sizing to avoid retransmissions and performance degradation. As a result, network engineers must account for these effects when designing GRE tunnels, often by implementing Path MTU Discovery or adjusting the MTU on tunnel interfaces.

Another significant aspect of GRE's operation within the OSI model is its interaction with the Control Plane and Data Plane mechanisms of modern routers and switches. While not part of the OSI model per se, the distinction between control and data planes maps loosely onto the model's layered architecture. The control plane, responsible for routing decisions and protocol negotiation, must be aware of GRE interfaces and treat them as valid routing destinations. The data plane, on the other hand, handles the actual forwarding of GRE-encapsulated packets, applying the appropriate encapsulation and decapsulation operations as traffic flows through the device. This layered interaction is crucial for ensuring the seamless operation of GRE in dynamic routing environments.

Ultimately, GRE's position in the OSI model provides valuable insight into how it functions and how it should be deployed. It acts as a transparent transport mechanism for encapsulated Layer 3 traffic, enabling flexible network designs that span diverse infrastructures. While its core operations are centered in the Network Layer, GRE's influence extends both upward and downward, affecting and depending on other layers to provide end-to-end connectivity. Understanding these interactions helps engineers implement GRE in a way that aligns with network design principles, maximizes performance, and ensures reliable communication across complex and distributed environments.

GRE Header Structure

The GRE header plays a central role in the functioning of Generic Routing Encapsulation, serving as the structure that allows entire packets to be encapsulated and transported across IP networks. Understanding the GRE header in detail is critical for engineers and network professionals who must design, troubleshoot, or optimize networks using GRE tunnels. Despite GRE's simplicity and elegance, the header format is highly flexible and capable of supporting a variety of use cases and optional features. The structure of the GRE header allows for efficient encapsulation of payloads while also enabling additional features such as tunnel identification, sequencing, and checksum verification. By examining the GRE header in its full detail, it becomes easier to appreciate how this protocol achieves its core function of creating virtual point-to-point links across diverse and often complex IP infrastructures.

At its most basic, the GRE header is composed of a fixed portion and an optional portion. The minimum GRE header is four bytes in length and contains essential control bits and a protocol type field. This minimal configuration is sufficient for the majority of GRE use cases, particularly those that do not require advanced tunnel management features. The first bits of the GRE header are reserved for flags, which are used to indicate the presence of optional fields. These flags include the Checksum Present (C), Routing Present (R), Key Present (K), Sequence Number Present (S), and Strict Source Route (s) bits. When set, each of these flags signals that additional fields are included in the GRE header, and the receiving device must interpret and process these fields accordingly. The flexibility of these control bits enables GRE to adapt its behavior based on the needs of the encapsulating application.

Following the flag bits, the GRE header includes a reserved section used for future expansion. Although these bits are typically set to zero, they offer a means of evolving the GRE protocol while maintaining backward compatibility. After the reserved section, the Protocol Type field identifies the type of payload encapsulated within the GRE packet. This field is two bytes long and corresponds to values in the Ethernet protocol type space. For example, if the payload is an IPv4 packet, the Protocol Type is set to 0x0800. If the payload is IPv6, the field is set to 0x86DD. This mechanism allows GRE to encapsulate not only IP-based traffic but also a variety of other Layer 3 protocols. By explicitly identifying the protocol type, the GRE header ensures that the receiving device can accurately interpret and decapsulate the payload.

When additional features are required, the GRE header expands to include optional fields such as the Key field and the Sequence Number field. The Key field is four bytes in length and is used to differentiate multiple GRE tunnels that exist between the same pair of endpoints. This is particularly useful in scenarios where multiple logical tunnels are established for different types of traffic or service levels. For example, in a multipoint GRE configuration or in dynamic multipoint VPNs (DMVPN), the Key field helps ensure that traffic is directed through the appropriate virtual circuit. The Key can also function as a rudimentary form of access control by acting as a shared secret known to both tunnel endpoints.

The Sequence Number field, also four bytes in length, provides a way to order packets as they traverse the GRE tunnel. This field is especially valuable when GRE is used over transport protocols that do not inherently guarantee in-order delivery. By assigning a unique sequence number to each encapsulated packet, the sending device enables the receiving device to detect lost, duplicated, or out-of-order packets. Although GRE does not inherently provide retransmission mechanisms, the sequence number allows upper-layer protocols or applications to handle such discrepancies if needed. The presence of the sequence number adds a layer of robustness in environments where packet delivery reliability is critical.

Another optional field is the Checksum field, which, when enabled, provides basic integrity checking for the GRE header and payload. The checksum is computed using a standard algorithm over the GRE header and encapsulated payload data. This field is not enabled by default because GRE often operates over reliable lower-layer protocols such as IP with IPsec, which already provides stronger integrity verification. However, in cases where GRE is used in less secure environments or where hardware offloading is unavailable, the checksum adds a measure of protection against corrupted packets.

In some rare implementations, GRE can include a Routing field that supports strict or loose source routing. However, this feature is largely deprecated and not commonly used in modern networks due to its complexity and limited applicability. Still, the existence of the Routing Present bit in the GRE header reflects the protocol's original design goal of extensibility and support for advanced routing scenarios. Over time, simpler and more robust solutions have emerged for these use cases, relegating GRE source routing to a legacy feature.

The overall flexibility of the GRE header structure ensures that it can accommodate both simple and complex use cases without excessive overhead. The minimal four-byte header is sufficient for basic encapsulation, while the optional fields can be added as needed to support more advanced tunneling requirements. This modularity is one of the reasons why GRE continues to be widely used, even as newer tunneling protocols emerge. It allows network engineers to deploy GRE in a wide range of environments—from lightweight site-to-site tunnels to complex, dynamic VPN topologies.

The GRE header's design also reflects a deep understanding of networking requirements across different environments. It offers just enough functionality to support advanced use cases without becoming bloated or difficult to implement. Whether transporting unicast IP packets, enabling multicast routing over tunnels, or providing foundational support for overlay networks, the GRE header structure is capable of adapting to meet the needs of evolving network architectures. By mastering the details of the GRE header, engineers gain a deeper appreciation of how encapsulated traffic behaves, how tunnels are formed and managed, and how to diagnose issues when they arise in real-world deployments. The GRE header, in its simplicity and extensibility, exemplifies the elegance of protocol design tailored for both present and future networking challenges.

Encapsulation and Decapsulation in GRE

Encapsulation and decapsulation are the fundamental processes that enable GRE to function as a tunneling protocol. These two mechanisms allow data packets to be transported across intermediate networks that do not natively understand or support the original payload protocol. GRE achieves this by encapsulating the original packet inside a new

GRE header and an outer IP header before transmission and then removing these headers on the receiving side to recover the original packet. This process makes it possible to create a virtual point-to-point link between two distant endpoints, regardless of the underlying infrastructure, making GRE an essential tool in virtual networking, multi-protocol support, and VPN construction.

The encapsulation process begins at the source router or device where a GRE tunnel is configured. When a packet destined for a remote network enters the router, the routing table determines that the next hop lies across a GRE tunnel. Instead of forwarding the packet in its original form, the device encapsulates the entire packet, including its Layer 3 headers and payload, within a GRE header. This GRE header, which may include optional fields such as a key or sequence number, serves to define the properties and behavior of the tunnel. Immediately following the GRE header, an outer IP header is added. This outer IP header contains the source and destination IP addresses of the GRE tunnel endpoints, which are typically public or routable IP addresses known to both devices.

At this point, the packet is ready for transmission across the intermediate network. The underlying IP infrastructure, including routers and switches along the path, is unaware of the encapsulated data's content. These intermediate devices simply route the GRE-encapsulated packet based on the outer IP header. This transparency is one of GRE's most powerful characteristics, as it enables disparate protocols and private addressing schemes to traverse the same public network without modification or interference. The encapsulated packet is treated as standard IP traffic, and the underlying network does not need to support the encapsulated protocol directly.

Once the GRE packet reaches the destination tunnel endpoint, the decapsulation process begins. The receiving device examines the outer IP header and recognizes that the packet is addressed to its GRE tunnel interface. It then strips off the outer IP header, revealing the GRE header. Based on the flags and fields present in this header, the device processes any optional information such as keys or sequence numbers. After interpreting the GRE header, the device removes it as well, ultimately exposing the original payload packet. This original packet is then forwarded based on its destination address, typically using standard routing decisions. To the higher layers of the network stack, it appears as though the packet arrived through a direct, point-to-point connection, even though it may have traversed a complex and extensive IP infrastructure.

This ability to encapsulate and decapsulate entire packets makes GRE a protocol-agnostic transport mechanism. Whether the original payload is IPv4, IPv6, or a less common protocol like IPX or AppleTalk, GRE can carry it through an IP-based network without alteration. This versatility has made GRE especially valuable in scenarios where legacy systems must interoperate with modern IP networks. The encapsulation process ensures that protocol-specific characteristics, addressing formats, and routing logic are preserved from end to end, allowing seamless communication between heterogeneous network segments.

GRE encapsulation does introduce additional overhead, which must be accounted for when designing the network. The combination of the GRE header and the outer IP header increases the overall size of the packet. Depending on the presence of optional GRE fields, this overhead can range from 24 to 36 bytes or more. If the resulting packet exceeds the maximum transmission unit (MTU) of the underlying network path, fragmentation may occur, which can degrade performance or cause connectivity issues if not properly managed. Techniques such as Path MTU Discovery and manual MTU adjustment on tunnel interfaces are often employed to mitigate these problems. Proper planning is essential to avoid packet loss, latency, or throughput reduction due to fragmentation or dropped packets.

In addition to affecting MTU, the encapsulation process also impacts security considerations. Because GRE itself does not provide encryption or authentication, the encapsulated data is potentially vulnerable to inspection or tampering as it traverses untrusted networks. To address this, GRE is often used in conjunction with IPsec. In this configuration, GRE performs the encapsulation function, and IPsec provides encryption and integrity protection. This layered approach allows engineers to benefit from GRE's flexibility and protocol support while ensuring that the traffic remains confidential and tamper-proof. The encapsulated GRE packet, once encrypted by

IPsec, can be safely transmitted over public networks such as the internet without exposing sensitive data or routing information.

GRE encapsulation is also central to the operation of dynamic routing protocols over tunnels. Protocols such as OSPF, EIGRP, and BGP often rely on multicast or broadcast traffic for neighbor discovery and routing updates. These types of traffic are not supported by native IPsec tunnels but are fully compatible with GRE. By encapsulating routing protocol packets inside GRE, engineers can ensure that dynamic routing functions correctly across the tunnel, enabling more flexible and resilient network designs. Once decapsulated, the routing packets are processed as if they had arrived on a direct physical interface, maintaining the expected behavior of the routing protocol.

Beyond basic tunneling, the encapsulation and decapsulation processes in GRE enable more advanced networking architectures. GRE is frequently used to build overlay networks, connect remote offices to data centers, and facilitate hybrid cloud deployments. It provides the abstraction necessary to unify different segments of an organization's infrastructure into a coherent and manageable network. Each GRE tunnel acts as a virtual wire that can carry any supported protocol, regardless of the physical topology or underlying routing domain.

In practice, encapsulation and decapsulation are seamless and automatic once the GRE tunnel is configured. The router or device managing the tunnel handles all aspects of the packet transformation, ensuring consistent delivery and routing transparency. This ease of operation is a key reason for GRE's enduring popularity. Engineers can create robust, scalable, and flexible network solutions using GRE without requiring significant changes to the existing network architecture. The processes of encapsulation and decapsulation, while technically simple, unlock a vast range of possibilities for network design, allowing complex routing and security requirements to be met with a single, lightweight protocol.

GRE vs Other Tunneling Protocols

Generic Routing Encapsulation, or GRE, is a tunneling protocol developed by Cisco that provides a mechanism to encapsulate a wide variety of network layer protocols inside point-to-point connections. GRE has become a fundamental tool in the world of networking, primarily because of its flexibility and broad support. However, GRE is not the only tunneling protocol available. There are several others such as IPsec, L2TP, MPLS, VXLAN, and WireGuard, each offering distinct features and trade-offs. A detailed comparison of GRE against these alternatives provides insight into its strengths and limitations, as well as the contexts in which it is most effective.

GRE is valued for its simplicity and protocol agnosticism. It can encapsulate any Layer 3 protocol, making it extremely versatile. This ability allows it to carry multicast traffic, such as routing protocol updates, over networks that do not natively support them. For example, GRE tunnels can be used to transport OSPF or EIGRP packets across an IP backbone that would otherwise drop these packets. This quality makes GRE an ideal candidate for creating VPN backbones, especially in multi-protocol environments. It also operates over IP, which means it can traverse virtually any IP-based infrastructure without significant issues.

However, one of GRE's significant limitations is its lack of inherent encryption or authentication mechanisms. By itself, GRE does not provide confidentiality or integrity protection. This is where IPsec often becomes a companion technology. IPsec is a suite of protocols designed specifically for securing IP communications by authenticating and encrypting each IP packet in a communication session. IPsec operates in two modes: transport mode and tunnel mode. In tunnel mode, which is often used in conjunction with GRE, the entire original IP packet is encrypted and encapsulated within a new IP packet. When GRE is combined with IPsec, it becomes a robust solution offering both protocol versatility and security.

Compared to IPsec as a standalone tunneling protocol, GRE appears more lightweight but far less secure. IPsec alone cannot encapsulate multicast or non-IP traffic, which is a point in GRE's favor. However, in environments where security is the top priority, IPsec's built-in encryption and integrity checks make it more suitable. Thus, GRE without IPsec is generally not advisable in situations where data confidentiality is a requirement, such as in public internet transport.

Another tunneling protocol often considered alongside GRE is Layer 2 Tunneling Protocol, or L2TP. L2TP is used to support virtual private networks or as part of the delivery of services by internet service providers. L2TP encapsulates Layer 2 frames and, much like GRE, lacks built-in encryption. As a result, it is frequently used with IPsec to provide secure VPN services. The main difference is that L2TP operates at Layer 2, making it suitable for scenarios where the tunneling of entire Ethernet frames is needed. GRE, on the other hand, operates at Layer 3, which restricts it to encapsulating IP packets and other Layer 3 protocols. This distinction makes L2TP more appropriate for certain enterprise and ISP scenarios that require full Layer 2 tunneling capabilities.

Multiprotocol Label Switching, or MPLS, represents a more sophisticated approach to tunneling. MPLS does not encapsulate packets in the traditional sense but instead uses labels to make forwarding decisions. MPLS tunnels, known as label-switched paths, offer high performance and are particularly effective in large-scale service provider environments. Unlike GRE, MPLS is deeply integrated into the service provider's infrastructure and offers traffic engineering, quality of service, and fast reroute capabilities. While GRE is more accessible and easier to deploy for small to medium-scale operations, MPLS offers unmatched scalability and performance optimization, though at the cost of complexity and vendor-specific dependencies.

More recently, protocols like VXLAN have emerged to address the challenges of tunneling in virtualized and cloud environments. VXLAN, or Virtual Extensible LAN, is designed to overcome the limitations of traditional VLANs, offering better scalability by using a 24-bit segment ID, known as the VXLAN Network Identifier. Unlike GRE, which encapsulates Layer 3 traffic, VXLAN encapsulates Layer 2 Ethernet frames in UDP packets, making it suitable for extending Layer 2 networks across Layer 3 infrastructure. VXLAN is heavily used in data center networks to support large-scale multi-tenant architectures and is well-suited for use in software-defined networking environments. While GRE remains relevant for traditional network interconnects, VXLAN is often the protocol of choice in virtualized environments due to its integration with modern orchestration tools and hypervisors.

WireGuard is a relatively new protocol that combines simplicity, high performance, and strong cryptography. Unlike GRE, WireGuard was built with security as a foundational principle. It provides encryption, authentication, and simplicity in configuration, making it ideal for point-to-point secure tunnels. WireGuard operates at Layer 3 and is significantly easier to audit and maintain than older protocols like IPsec. Despite being new, it has quickly gained traction due to its small codebase and efficiency. In comparison, GRE's lack of security features requires it to be paired with other protocols to offer similar levels of confidentiality, which increases complexity. WireGuard, therefore, can be a compelling alternative to GRE in secure networking scenarios where ease of use and strong encryption are priorities.

Ultimately, GRE continues to be a vital part of the network engineer's toolkit because of its protocol flexibility and ease of deployment. It shines in scenarios where encapsulation of non-IP protocols or multicast traffic is required, and where encryption is either unnecessary or handled by other layers. However, in a landscape filled with modern tunneling protocols that offer built-in security, scalability, or virtualization support, GRE must often be paired with complementary technologies to remain competitive. Understanding the specific strengths and limitations of each tunneling protocol is essential when designing resilient, secure, and efficient network infrastructures.

GRE over IP and IP-in-IP Differences

In the realm of network tunneling protocols, GRE over IP and IP-in-IP encapsulation serve as two widely used techniques for encapsulating packets and enabling communication across routed or incompatible networks. While they may appear similar on the surface, both involving the encapsulation of IP packets within another IP packet, their structures, use cases, and capabilities differ in meaningful ways. Understanding the nuances between GRE over IP and IP-in-IP is essential for network engineers and architects who are tasked with designing efficient and flexible networks. Both protocols operate at the network layer and involve adding new IP headers to encapsulate payloads, but their behaviors, headers, and extensibility differ significantly.

IP-in-IP, sometimes referred to as IPIP, is a straightforward encapsulation method that allows an IP packet to be wrapped within another IP packet. This method was defined in RFC 2003 and was primarily designed to tunnel one IP network through another IP network. The encapsulation adds a new IP header in front of the original packet, preserving the entire original IP packet as the payload. The outer IP header contains the source and destination IP addresses of the tunnel endpoints, while the inner IP header remains untouched and visible only after the decapsulation process. This method is simple and introduces minimal overhead since it adds only one additional 20-byte IPv4 header or 40-byte IPv6 header. Its simplicity, however, comes at the cost of flexibility. IP-in-IP can only encapsulate IP packets and does not support non-IP protocols or multicast traffic. This limitation restricts its use in environments where protocols such as OSPF or EIGRP need to be tunneled across IP networks, especially when those protocols rely on multicast for neighbor discovery or updates.

In contrast, GRE, or Generic Routing Encapsulation, was developed by Cisco and later standardized in RFC 2784 and RFC 2890. GRE is a more versatile tunneling protocol that enables the encapsulation of a wide range of network layer protocols, not just IP. GRE over IP refers to the method of encapsulating any Layer 3 protocol within a GRE header, which itself is then encapsulated within an IP packet. This dual-layer encapsulation allows GRE to support non-IP protocols, multicast, and even bridged Ethernet traffic under certain implementations. The GRE header adds 4 bytes in its basic form, but optional fields such as checksums, keys, or sequence numbers can increase the header size. The added GRE header provides greater control and flexibility, including optional features like identifying different tunnels with key fields or maintaining order with sequence numbers. These features are unavailable in the IP-in-IP model, making GRE the better choice in scenarios where additional control or multi-protocol support is necessary.

One of the key differences lies in their support for routing protocols. Since IP-in-IP does not support the encapsulation of multicast traffic, it cannot be used to tunnel routing protocols that rely on multicast packets to function. GRE, however, can encapsulate such traffic, allowing protocols like OSPF or EIGRP to work across disjointed IP networks. This makes GRE especially useful in enterprise environments where dynamic routing needs to be maintained across VPN tunnels or where direct Layer 2 connectivity does not exist. Additionally, GRE can be used to carry non-IP payloads, such as AppleTalk or Internetwork Packet Exchange (IPX), although such use cases are less common in modern networks. The ability to support multiple protocols makes GRE a powerful option for building virtual private networks or overlay networks in multi-vendor or legacy environments.

In terms of configuration and processing complexity, IP-in-IP is generally simpler to implement and manage. Its smaller overhead and limited scope of functionality result in lower processing requirements for routers and network devices. Because it only deals with IP packets and does not introduce optional fields or complex encapsulation logic, it is often preferred in scenarios where performance and simplicity are paramount. GRE, by comparison, requires more resources due to its additional header and optional features. Devices handling GRE traffic must be capable of processing GRE headers, parsing optional fields, and managing multiple tunnels that may be identified by key fields. This increased processing demand may be a consideration in high-throughput environments or on devices with limited CPU or memory resources.

Another important difference is interoperability and standardization. Both GRE and IP-in-IP are supported on a wide range of devices and platforms, but GRE enjoys broader support due to its long-standing association with Cisco and its versatility. Most modern operating systems, routers, and firewalls include support for both protocols, but GRE tends to be the more commonly used tunneling method in enterprise deployments. Its compatibility with IPsec for securing traffic also gives it a distinct advantage. While IP-in-IP can theoretically be protected with IPsec as well, GRE is more often paired with IPsec in real-world deployments to create secure and versatile VPN tunnels that can carry both unicast and multicast traffic.

Ultimately, the decision to use GRE over IP or IP-in-IP comes down to the specific requirements of the network environment. For simple encapsulation of unicast IP traffic across incompatible IP networks, IP-in-IP provides a lightweight and efficient solution. For more complex scenarios that involve routing protocols, multicast traffic, or non-IP protocols, GRE over IP offers the necessary flexibility and control. Each protocol has its own strengths, and understanding these differences ensures that network professionals can make informed decisions when designing and implementing tunneling solutions. Whether it is for connecting remote sites, supporting virtualized infrastructures, or building scalable overlay networks, choosing the appropriate tunneling method can significantly impact the performance, reliability, and maintainability of the network architecture.

Configuration Basics of GRE Tunnels

Configuring a GRE tunnel involves several key steps that must be executed with precision to ensure a stable and functional encapsulated connection between two endpoints. GRE, or Generic Routing Encapsulation, operates by taking packets of one protocol and encapsulating them inside the packets of another protocol, allowing for the transport of data across incompatible or disjointed network infrastructures. This process is particularly useful when two networks need to be logically connected over a third-party or public IP backbone, such as the internet, without altering the existing internal addressing or routing configurations. Understanding how to set up a GRE tunnel from a configuration perspective requires familiarity with IP addressing, routing, and basic tunneling principles.

The first and most essential step in configuring a GRE tunnel is the identification of the tunnel endpoints. Each endpoint must have a reachable public IP address that can serve as the outer header's source and destination. These are the IP addresses that will be used in the outer IP header to route the encapsulated packets across the intervening network. Without proper IP connectivity between the two endpoints, the GRE tunnel will not form. Therefore, it is often necessary to ensure that the physical or underlying transport infrastructure, whether it is MPLS, broadband, or a simple IP link, is functional and stable before any GRE configuration is attempted.

Once the endpoints are determined and verified for reachability, the GRE tunnel interface must be created. This logical interface is configured on both routers or devices that will participate in the tunnel. The tunnel interface is assigned a virtual IP address that represents the inner IP header of the GRE tunnel. This IP address is not related to the physical interface's IP address and is used by routing protocols or static routes to determine how traffic should be sent through the tunnel. Typically, the tunnel interface is assigned an IP address from a unique subnet that is shared between both tunnel endpoints, effectively creating a point-to-point network overlaid on top of the public infrastructure.

The next step involves specifying the source and destination for the tunnel. These are defined as the public IP addresses of the respective tunnel endpoints. The tunnel source is usually a physical or loopback interface on the local router, while the tunnel destination is the remote endpoint's IP address. These values instruct the router how to encapsulate outgoing packets into GRE and where to send them. The source and destination configuration must be symmetrical; otherwise, the GRE tunnel will fail to establish. It is critical to ensure that the tunnel source and destination are properly routable across the intervening network. In many implementations, administrators will prefer to use loopback interfaces as tunnel sources because they offer greater stability and do not change even if physical interfaces fail.

With the tunnel interface, source, and destination configured, routing must be enabled over the GRE tunnel. This can be achieved by using static routes or dynamic routing protocols such as OSPF, EIGRP, or BGP. These protocols can treat the GRE tunnel as just another IP interface, allowing for seamless integration into the overall network topology. One of the primary advantages of GRE is its ability to carry multicast traffic, which means that dynamic routing protocols that rely on multicast can function properly over the tunnel. This is a significant advantage over simpler encapsulation techniques like IP-in-IP, which only support unicast traffic. Routing configuration ensures that the network can intelligently decide which traffic should be sent through the tunnel, and it allows for redundancy, failover, and route optimization when multiple tunnels are present.

While the basic GRE configuration is relatively straightforward, it is important to consider optional enhancements and troubleshooting tools. For instance, GRE tunnels do not include native encryption or authentication. If secure transport is required, GRE is often paired with IPsec to protect the encapsulated traffic. In such configurations, IPsec provides confidentiality, integrity, and authentication, while GRE provides the encapsulation functionality and protocol versatility. This combination allows for secure transmission of dynamic routing protocols and multicast traffic over untrusted networks such as the public internet. Configuring GRE over IPsec typically involves defining crypto maps or IPsec profiles and applying them to the tunnel interface, depending on the specific router platform or operating system.

GRE tunnels can also benefit from features such as tunnel keepalives or bidirectional forwarding detection (BFD). These mechanisms are used to monitor the health of the GRE tunnel and detect failures more quickly than traditional routing protocol timers. Tunnel keepalives involve sending periodic messages across the tunnel, and if responses are not received, the tunnel is marked as down. This proactive monitoring improves network convergence and can prevent black holes in routing, where traffic is sent into a non-functional tunnel interface.

Another important aspect of GRE configuration is managing the maximum transmission unit (MTU). Because GRE adds additional headers to the original packet, the overall packet size increases. If this size exceeds the MTU of the underlying physical interface or the path MTU between endpoints, fragmentation may occur. Fragmentation can degrade performance and lead to packet loss, particularly if ICMP messages used for Path MTU Discovery are blocked. Administrators can mitigate this issue by adjusting the MTU or the maximum segment size (MSS) on tunnel interfaces or by configuring devices to avoid generating packets that exceed the MTU.

Logging and monitoring play an essential role in the ongoing maintenance of GRE tunnels. Debugging tools and commands such as traceroute, ping, and interface statistics can help administrators confirm the tunnel's operational status and detect potential misconfigurations. Logs may reveal issues such as unreachable destinations, incorrect IP addresses, or problems related to IPsec if encryption is in use. Careful observation of these logs during and after configuration can prevent prolonged outages and ensure the tunnel functions as intended.

Overall, setting up a GRE tunnel involves a sequence of well-defined steps that must be completed accurately. From selecting tunnel endpoints and configuring interfaces to integrating routing and optional security measures, each phase contributes to the tunnel's stability and functionality. The configurability and protocol flexibility of GRE make it a powerful tool in a network engineer's arsenal, allowing disparate networks to be connected in a logical and scalable manner across virtually any IP-based transport infrastructure.

Static Routing over GRE Tunnels

Implementing static routing over GRE tunnels is a foundational technique in network design, particularly in environments where simplicity, predictability, and administrative control are prioritized. GRE, or Generic Routing Encapsulation, creates a virtual point-to-point connection between two routers by encapsulating packets in a new IP header. This encapsulation allows for the transportation of various Layer 3 protocols, including multicast and non-IP traffic, across an IP-based network. When static routing is layered on top of this GRE tunnel, administrators can dictate the exact path that traffic should follow without relying on dynamic routing protocols. This combination is commonly used in branch office connectivity, hub-and-spoke topologies, or in scenarios where the overhead of dynamic routing is unnecessary or undesired.

At its core, static routing over a GRE tunnel requires the manual definition of routes that direct specific traffic through the virtual tunnel interface. After a GRE tunnel is properly configured and operational between two endpoints, the next step is to inform the router how to send packets toward remote networks that exist on the other side of the tunnel. This is achieved by creating static routes that point to the tunnel interface as the next hop or use the tunnel's remote IP address as the route destination. These static routes ensure that any packets destined for specific networks are encapsulated inside the GRE tunnel and transported across the IP network to reach the intended destination.

The process begins by identifying the network prefixes that must be reached through the GRE tunnel. These could be networks in a remote branch office, in another data center, or even in a cloud environment, depending on the deployment. On the local router, a static route is added to the routing table, indicating that to reach a particular remote network, packets should be forwarded via the GRE tunnel interface. The router, upon receiving traffic destined for that network, will encapsulate it using the GRE format and then transmit it through the outer IP layer to the remote GRE endpoint. Upon arrival, the remote router decapsulates the GRE packet, extracts the original payload, and forwards it internally based on its own routing table.

Static routing is appealing in GRE tunnel deployments for several reasons. First, it offers administrative control and determinism. Because the routes are manually configured, there is no dependence on neighbor discovery, protocol convergence, or routing advertisements. This predictability is useful in stable environments where the network topology does not change frequently. It also simplifies security and troubleshooting since the routing behavior is fully defined by the administrator and not influenced by potentially misconfigured or rogue routing peers. In regulatory or compliance-driven networks, static routing can also help ensure traffic paths remain predictable and auditable.

Another key advantage of static routing over GRE is that it introduces very little overhead compared to dynamic routing protocols. Without the need to maintain routing adjacencies, exchange routing updates, or process protocol-specific metrics, routers consume fewer resources. This efficiency can be crucial in resource-constrained environments such as low-power routers in remote offices or edge devices in industrial settings. Additionally, static routing reduces the attack surface, as there are no routing protocol messages that can be intercepted, spoofed, or manipulated by an attacker.

Despite its simplicity, static routing over GRE does require careful planning and consistent configuration. Both tunnel endpoints must have matching static routes pointing to the appropriate destination networks, or else return traffic will not be properly delivered. If a static route is missing on one side, packets may be successfully forwarded in one direction but dropped on the return path, creating a frustrating and hard-to-diagnose asymmetric routing scenario. For this reason, network administrators must ensure that each router participating in the GRE tunnel is configured with reciprocal static routes that accurately reflect the network topology.

Redundancy and failover represent areas where static routing is less flexible compared to dynamic routing. Because static routes do not adjust automatically to changes in network state, a tunnel failure or path disruption may cause traffic black holes unless additional mechanisms are implemented. To mitigate this risk, some network designs pair GRE tunnels with tunnel keepalives or Bidirectional Forwarding Detection (BFD), which can detect tunnel failures and trigger route removal or failover logic via routing policy or scripting. Alternatively, administrators may configure floating static routes with higher administrative distances that only activate if primary routes become unavailable. While this introduces a measure of adaptability, it still does not provide the level of responsiveness and automatic convergence found in dynamic routing protocols.

Another important consideration when using static routing over GRE is scalability. In small deployments with only a few tunnels and networks, managing static routes is straightforward. However, as the number of tunnels, branches, or remote prefixes grows, the administrative burden increases rapidly. Each new network requires a manual update to the static routing table on each participating router, which increases the potential for configuration errors and inconsistency. In large-scale environments, this manual overhead can become unsustainable, prompting a shift toward hybrid designs where static routing is used for core backbone tunnels and dynamic routing is used to manage edge networks more flexibly.

Despite these challenges, static routing remains a powerful and viable solution for many GRE tunnel applications. It offers clarity, simplicity, and precise control, making it an excellent choice for stable environments where network paths are fixed and unlikely to change frequently. For service providers or enterprises that require tightly managed traffic flows or need to implement strict segmentation between departments, partners, or services, static routes over GRE tunnels provide a reliable and transparent mechanism to enforce those boundaries.

Static routing over GRE tunnels also integrates well with other technologies such as IPsec. When GRE is used to encapsulate traffic and IPsec is applied for security, the use of static routes helps keep the configuration manageable. Since the tunnel endpoints and routes are fixed, there is no need to dynamically negotiate policies for multiple prefixes, which simplifies the overall IPsec configuration. In such deployments, static routes serve not only to guide traffic but also to enforce specific traffic patterns that align with security and performance objectives.

Ultimately, static routing over GRE tunnels offers a compelling solution for many practical networking challenges. Its strengths lie in its simplicity, predictability, and ease of implementation, making it ideal for controlled and well-defined network topologies. While it may not scale effortlessly in large or highly dynamic environments, it provides a strong foundation for connectivity where flexibility and automation are secondary to stability and control. Through careful design and disciplined configuration, static routes can enable reliable communication over GRE tunnels, delivering connectivity that is both efficient and secure.

Dynamic Routing over GRE Tunnels

Dynamic routing over GRE tunnels is a widely adopted approach in modern networking environments that require flexibility, scalability, and resilience. Unlike static routing, which relies on manually configured paths, dynamic routing allows routers to automatically discover, advertise, and adapt to network changes using standardized routing protocols. When deployed over GRE tunnels, dynamic routing brings enhanced capabilities to otherwise rigid tunneling solutions, enabling efficient traffic forwarding, automated failover, and simplified management of complex topologies. GRE tunnels themselves are inherently protocol-agnostic and capable of carrying multicast and broadcast traffic, which is essential for the proper functioning of many dynamic routing protocols that rely on such traffic to form neighbor adjacencies and share routing information.

To enable dynamic routing over GRE tunnels, network engineers typically configure a routing protocol such as OSPF, EIGRP, or BGP on the virtual tunnel interface. Once the GRE tunnel is established and operational, the routing protocol treats the tunnel as just another IP link. This allows routers at each endpoint to form neighbor relationships, exchange routes, and populate their routing tables with information about networks that lie beyond the GRE tunnel. The routing protocol sees the GRE tunnel interface as a direct connection to the peer, unaware of the underlying IP backbone that transports the encapsulated packets. This abstraction simplifies the design and hides the complexity of the physical or transport-layer infrastructure beneath the GRE layer.

One of the most commonly used protocols for dynamic routing over GRE tunnels is OSPF. OSPF's support for areas, cost metrics, and link-state advertisements makes it well-suited for deployment in hierarchical enterprise networks. When OSPF is configured over a GRE tunnel, the tunnel interface must be assigned an IP address, and the OSPF process must include that interface in its configuration. Once both ends of the tunnel are configured correctly, OSPF forms an adjacency and begins exchanging LSAs to build the network topology. This process allows for automatic route learning and propagation across multiple sites, greatly reducing administrative overhead. Additionally, OSPF can detect changes in the network and recalculate best paths, ensuring that traffic is routed efficiently even in the event of failures or topology changes.

EIGRP is another protocol well-suited for dynamic routing over GRE tunnels, especially in Cisco-centric environments. EIGRP's rapid convergence, use of composite metrics, and ease of configuration make it a practical choice for environments where performance and reliability are critical. Like OSPF, EIGRP can form adjacencies over GRE tunnels and exchange routing information using multicast packets, which GRE supports. The ability of GRE to carry multicast traffic is what enables dynamic routing protocols to function properly, distinguishing GRE from simpler tunneling techniques such as IP-in-

IP, which only support unicast traffic. EIGRP's support for unequal-cost load balancing adds another layer of efficiency, allowing network administrators to make better use of available bandwidth across multiple GRE tunnels.

BGP, the protocol that powers the global internet, is also frequently deployed over GRE tunnels in large-scale networks, such as service provider backbones, data centers, and multi-tenant environments. BGP's scalability and policy-driven routing model make it ideal for scenarios where routing control, traffic engineering, and route filtering are necessary. When BGP is used over GRE, the tunnel interface is configured with appropriate IP addresses, and BGP peerings are established using those addresses. Because BGP does not rely on multicast to form neighbor relationships, it can operate even over tunnels that do not support multicast traffic. However, using BGP over GRE still provides the benefits of abstracting the transport infrastructure and allowing for interconnection of routing domains across intermediate IP networks.

One of the most significant benefits of dynamic routing over GRE tunnels is the automatic adaptation to network changes. When a link or tunnel goes down, dynamic routing protocols detect the failure through timers, keepalives, or advanced features like Bidirectional Forwarding Detection (BFD). They then recalculate the routing table and select an alternate path if available. This capability is critical in high-availability environments where uninterrupted connectivity is a requirement. Dynamic routing protocols ensure that traffic is rerouted around failed links without manual intervention, greatly enhancing the network's resilience and uptime.

Scalability is another compelling reason to use dynamic routing over GRE tunnels. In networks with many branches, data centers, or cloud regions, manually managing static routes quickly becomes infeasible. Dynamic routing allows each site to advertise its networks and learn about others without needing to explicitly define every possible route. This automatic propagation of route information simplifies configuration and ongoing maintenance. It also enables the use of summarization, route filtering, and redistribution to maintain efficient and manageable routing tables, which is especially valuable as networks grow in size and complexity.

Despite its advantages, deploying dynamic routing over GRE tunnels is not without challenges. Proper configuration is crucial to avoid routing loops, suboptimal paths, or flapping adjacencies. Careful attention must be paid to route metrics, interface costs, and protocol-specific timers. In some cases, the use of GRE may result in lower throughput due to encapsulation overhead, which slightly increases packet size and can lead to fragmentation if not properly managed. Adjustments to the maximum transmission unit (MTU) or maximum segment size (MSS) may be necessary to prevent performance degradation. Path MTU discovery should also be considered to optimize packet delivery and avoid issues caused by intermediate devices dropping oversized packets.

Security is another consideration when implementing dynamic routing over GRE tunnels. Because GRE does not provide encryption or authentication, the tunnel traffic is vulnerable to interception or manipulation if traversing untrusted networks. To address this risk, GRE is often paired with IPsec, which secures the encapsulated traffic with encryption, authentication, and integrity checks. In such deployments, routing protocols continue to operate over the GRE interface, unaware that IPsec is providing the security. This separation of duties allows for powerful combinations of routing flexibility and transport-layer security.

Dynamic routing over GRE tunnels enables the creation of highly adaptable and resilient network architectures. Whether connecting remote sites, building overlay networks, or supporting complex cloud hybrid environments, this approach provides the means to scale routing dynamically while maintaining logical separation and control. By leveraging GRE's encapsulation capabilities and the intelligence of routing protocols, network engineers can construct robust infrastructures capable of responding automatically to failures, topology changes, and evolving traffic patterns. The synergy between GRE and dynamic routing remains a cornerstone of enterprise and service provider network designs, delivering both efficiency and operational simplicity in diverse deployment scenarios.

GRE with OSPF Integration

Integrating GRE with OSPF creates a powerful solution for building scalable, flexible, and dynamic networks across disparate IP infrastructures. GRE, or Generic Routing Encapsulation, enables the encapsulation of packets from various Layer 3 protocols, including IP multicast and broadcast traffic, which are essential for dynamic routing protocol operations. OSPF, or Open Shortest Path First, is a link-state interior gateway protocol designed for dynamic routing within an autonomous system. When GRE tunnels are combined with OSPF, administrators gain the ability to establish routing adjacencies across IP networks that would otherwise block or drop multicast packets. This integration allows for the seamless extension of routing domains, even across public or intermediate networks that do not natively support dynamic routing traffic.

The synergy between GRE and OSPF begins with the establishment of the GRE tunnel itself. A GRE tunnel creates a virtual point-to-point link between two routers, overlaying the existing IP infrastructure. This virtual link is treated as a standard interface by OSPF, which then forms neighbor relationships and exchanges routing information as if the two endpoints were directly connected. The GRE tunnel encapsulates OSPF's multicast hello packets, enabling them to traverse networks that are inherently unicast only, such as the internet or MPLS backbones. This makes GRE an ideal mechanism for extending OSPF's reach beyond local LANs or across complex, multi-vendor infrastructures.

Once the GRE tunnel is configured and operational, the next step involves enabling OSPF on the tunnel interface. This requires assigning IP addresses to the tunnel endpoints and including those addresses in the OSPF configuration under the appropriate process and area. The OSPF hello and dead intervals must match on both sides to ensure neighbor adjacency is successfully established. After the adjacency is formed, the routers begin exchanging link-state advertisements, allowing each device to build a complete picture of the network topology. Routes learned through OSPF over GRE tunnels are then installed in the routing table and used to forward traffic to remote networks.

One of the key benefits of using OSPF over GRE is the ability to extend OSPF areas across networks that would otherwise be opaque to dynamic routing. For example, two branch offices connected via a public internet link can appear to be part of the same OSPF area if joined through a GRE tunnel. This creates a logical topology that matches the desired routing architecture, regardless of the physical constraints of the underlying network. Such designs can reduce complexity in large enterprises by maintaining a unified routing protocol and consistent policy framework across distributed sites.

GRE and OSPF integration also supports multi-area OSPF deployments. A GRE tunnel can connect routers in different OSPF areas, serving as a backbone link or inter-area transit path. This is especially useful in hub-and-spoke topologies where branch routers connect back to a central data center. Each branch can be placed in its own OSPF area, while the central router operates in Area 0, the OSPF backbone. GRE tunnels from each branch to the central router ensure full reachability and efficient route summarization, enhancing scalability and simplifying troubleshooting.

Another advantage of integrating GRE with OSPF is the ability to support dynamic failover and load balancing. OSPF continuously monitors the state of links and recalculates best paths using the shortest path first algorithm. If a GRE tunnel fails or becomes unreachable, OSPF automatically recalculates routes and redirects traffic through alternate paths if available. This dynamic behavior enhances the resilience of the network without requiring manual intervention. Furthermore, OSPF supports equal-cost multipath routing (ECMP), allowing multiple GRE tunnels with identical metrics to be used simultaneously for load balancing, thereby improving bandwidth utilization and reducing latency.

The use of GRE with OSPF also allows administrators to control the routing domain and isolate routing updates. GRE tunnels create defined boundaries for OSPF advertisements, allowing for clear segmentation between OSPF areas or between different autonomous systems when route redistribution is involved. For example, in a managed services scenario, a provider can use GRE to deliver OSPF connectivity to customer sites without exposing the internal structure of its backbone. By encapsulating the routing information within GRE tunnels, the provider ensures clean separation of control planes, which is vital for operational security and scalability.

Despite the benefits, integrating GRE with OSPF requires careful planning to avoid performance and stability issues. GRE introduces additional header overhead, which increases packet size and can lead to fragmentation if not managed properly. Network administrators must ensure that the MTU on tunnel interfaces is configured appropriately and that path MTU discovery functions correctly across the underlying network. Failure to do so can result in packet loss or reduced throughput, undermining the reliability of routing adjacencies and the stability of the OSPF topology.

The configuration of GRE with OSPF must also account for redundancy and monitoring. Tunnel interfaces should be equipped with keepalive mechanisms or bidirectional forwarding detection to quickly detect failures. OSPF's default timers may not detect failures quickly enough in time-sensitive environments, so tuning hello and dead intervals can improve responsiveness. In highly available networks, redundant GRE tunnels can be created and included in the OSPF topology with appropriate cost metrics to control traffic flow and failover behavior. These measures ensure that the GRE and OSPF integration maintains high availability and fault tolerance, even in the face of network disruptions.

Security is another critical consideration. GRE itself provides no encryption or authentication, which makes it vulnerable to eavesdropping or tampering if the tunnel traverses untrusted networks. To mitigate this risk, GRE tunnels are often encapsulated within IPsec. When GRE over IPsec is combined with OSPF, the resulting configuration supports secure, dynamic, and resilient routing across insecure networks. IPsec handles confidentiality and integrity, while GRE supports multicast transport, and OSPF ensures dynamic route learning. This layered design is particularly effective in branch-to-branch or branch-to-hub deployments across the public internet, where security and dynamic routing must coexist.

Integrating GRE with OSPF empowers network architects to extend, scale, and secure dynamic routing domains across heterogeneous infrastructures. By leveraging the strengths of both technologies, networks can be built with flexibility, adaptability, and robustness. From connecting remote offices to centralizing dynamic routing across disparate platforms, the GRE and OSPF combination remains a cornerstone of modern network design. It allows routing protocols to function transparently across non-native environments and ensures that IP reachability and route optimization are preserved even across complex or segmented topologies. The ability to dynamically exchange routes, recover from failures, and maintain logical topologies across physical boundaries makes GRE with OSPF an indispensable tool in enterprise and service provider networks alike.

GRE with EIGRP Integration

Integrating GRE with EIGRP creates a powerful combination for dynamic routing across logically extended networks, especially in environments where control, scalability, and routing efficiency are critical. GRE, or Generic Routing Encapsulation, is a tunneling protocol that allows encapsulation of a wide range of Layer 3 traffic, including multicast and broadcast packets. These capabilities make GRE particularly suitable for transporting dynamic routing protocols like EIGRP, which rely on multicast messages to discover neighbors and exchange routing information. EIGRP, or Enhanced Interior Gateway Routing Protocol, is a Cisco proprietary distance-vector routing protocol that offers fast convergence, loop-free paths, and support for complex network topologies. When GRE is used in conjunction with EIGRP, the result is a robust and flexible routing solution capable of spanning diverse network infrastructures, including public IP networks and third-party backbones.

The integration process begins with the configuration of GRE tunnels between participating routers. GRE creates virtual point-to-point links that encapsulate packets inside IP headers, allowing them to traverse networks that do not natively support EIGRP's multicast traffic. These GRE tunnels act as logical interfaces that can be assigned IP addresses and treated like any physical interface by EIGRP. Once the GRE tunnel is established and operational, the EIGRP process is activated on the tunnel interface, enabling the formation of EIGRP neighbor relationships over the virtual link. This setup allows routers separated by an intermediate network to exchange routing information as if they were directly connected on the same physical link.

One of the key advantages of using GRE with EIGRP is the ability to build scalable and flexible network topologies that are not limited by the physical layout of the infrastructure. In traditional networks, EIGRP neighbor relationships require Layer 2 adjacency or multicast support, which may not be available across the public internet or within MPLS transport networks. GRE overcomes this limitation by encapsulating EIGRP's multicast hello packets, enabling them to reach the intended neighbor over an IP-based backbone. This allows enterprises to connect remote offices, data centers, or cloud environments into a unified EIGRP domain, regardless of the underlying network constraints.

Once EIGRP is operational over the GRE tunnel, routers begin exchanging routing updates and topology information using the Diffusing Update Algorithm (DUAL), which is EIGRP's core mechanism for ensuring loop-free, efficient routing decisions. EIGRP calculates the best path to each destination based on a composite metric that considers bandwidth, delay, reliability, and load. When GRE tunnels are part of the topology, these metrics include the characteristics of the tunnel interface, which can be adjusted to influence routing behavior. For example, an administrator may manipulate the delay or bandwidth values on the GRE tunnel to prefer one tunnel over another, enabling traffic engineering and route optimization within the EIGRP domain.

Another benefit of using EIGRP with GRE is support for unequal-cost load balancing. Unlike many routing protocols that only support equal-cost multipath, EIGRP allows traffic to be distributed across multiple paths with varying costs, provided that the paths meet the feasibility condition. When multiple GRE tunnels exist between sites, EIGRP can leverage this capability to balance traffic intelligently, improving bandwidth utilization and fault tolerance. This is particularly valuable in hub-and-spoke or full-mesh topologies where multiple paths may exist between locations.

Reliability and resilience are also enhanced by the dynamic nature of EIGRP. If a GRE tunnel fails due to loss of connectivity between endpoints, EIGRP detects the failure through the absence of hello packets or through triggered updates. Once a failure is detected, DUAL recalculates the best path to each destination and installs new routes in the forwarding table. This rapid convergence helps maintain continuous communication and minimizes the impact of failures. In high-availability environments, redundant GRE tunnels can be pre-configured, and EIGRP will automatically switch to backup tunnels when necessary, ensuring uninterrupted service.

Security is an important consideration when deploying EIGRP over GRE tunnels. Because GRE lacks native encryption or authentication, the encapsulated traffic, including EIGRP routing information, is susceptible to interception or manipulation if the tunnel traverses untrusted networks. To mitigate this risk, GRE is often paired with IPsec, which encrypts the GRE payload and ensures its confidentiality and integrity. When GRE over IPsec is combined with EIGRP, the network benefits from dynamic routing, flexible tunneling, and strong security, making it ideal for enterprise WANs, site-to-site VPNs, or multi-tenant infrastructures.

Proper configuration and planning are essential to ensure a stable EIGRP over GRE deployment. Tunnel endpoints must have reachable public or private IP addresses, and the underlying transport network must support the encapsulated traffic without excessive latency, loss, or MTU issues. The GRE tunnel interfaces should have appropriate MTU settings to avoid fragmentation, especially when IPsec is involved, as additional headers increase the overall packet size. Administrators must also monitor EIGRP metrics and ensure consistent route summarization, filtering, and redistribution practices, particularly when integrating GRE-based routes with other parts of the network.

GRE with EIGRP integration also supports complex topologies such as route reflectors, stub areas, and policy-based routing. For example, in a hub-and-spoke deployment, each spoke router can establish a GRE tunnel with the hub, and EIGRP can be configured to recognize the hub as the primary route distributor. Policies can be implemented to restrict spoke-to-spoke communication or to enforce preferred data paths. In full-mesh designs, each router may have GRE tunnels to

43

multiple peers, and EIGRP can dynamically determine the best path for each prefix based on real-time network conditions.

The integration also simplifies the deployment of new sites or services. Once a GRE tunnel is created and EIGRP is enabled, the new router automatically participates in the EIGRP routing domain and learns about the rest of the network without additional configuration. This plug-and-play approach reduces administrative overhead and accelerates provisioning in dynamic environments. Combined with modern network management tools, EIGRP over GRE tunnels can be monitored, tuned, and visualized to maintain optimal performance and uptime.

GRE with EIGRP creates a highly adaptable and efficient routing solution that extends the benefits of dynamic routing across infrastructure boundaries. It empowers organizations to build overlay networks that preserve routing intelligence and topology awareness while leveraging the flexibility of IP-based transport. Whether connecting remote branches, integrating cloud services, or unifying geographically dispersed locations, the combination of GRE and EIGRP provides a robust platform for scalable, secure, and automated network connectivity. Through careful configuration, monitoring, and design, network architects can use this integration to deliver seamless routing experiences that adapt to growth, change, and operational demands.

GRE with BGP Integration

Integrating GRE with BGP provides a versatile and scalable solution for interconnecting networks across diverse infrastructures, especially in multi-provider, inter-autonomous system, or hybrid cloud environments. GRE, or Generic Routing Encapsulation, creates a virtual point-to-point link between two endpoints by encapsulating network layer packets inside a new IP header, allowing protocols that rely on broadcast or multicast to traverse networks that do not support those types of traffic natively. BGP, or Border Gateway Protocol, is the protocol that underpins the global internet and is designed to exchange routing and reachability information between autonomous systems. When GRE is combined with BGP, network engineers can extend BGP peerings across non-directly connected IP networks while maintaining logical topologies that align with policy, security, and traffic engineering requirements.

The integration of GRE with BGP typically begins with the configuration of a GRE tunnel between two routers that belong to separate networks or autonomous systems. The GRE tunnel creates a logical interface on each router, assigned with IP addresses that are used as the source and destination of BGP sessions. Since BGP does not require multicast to establish peerings, it can operate over GRE tunnels just as it would over physical interfaces. The primary benefit of using GRE in this scenario is that it provides a stable and consistent path over which the BGP session can be established, even if the physical path between the routers traverses multiple intermediate networks, public IP space, or firewalls. This decouples the control plane relationship between BGP peers from the unpredictability of the underlying physical or IP infrastructure.

One of the most compelling use cases for GRE with BGP integration is in multi-provider environments, where organizations need to establish BGP sessions with partners, upstream providers, or remote data centers across public IP networks. GRE provides a secure and manageable overlay that encapsulates BGP traffic, allowing the peer relationship to be formed without exposing the underlying transport details. This is particularly useful in scenarios where the remote peer is located behind a NAT or firewall, and direct BGP peering is not possible. By using GRE tunnels, organizations can tunnel BGP packets through intermediate devices and treat the peer as if it were directly connected.

GRE with BGP is also widely used in MPLS VPN environments, where the core of the network may be entirely IP-based, and GRE is used to carry BGP sessions between Provider Edge (PE) routers or between Customer Edge (CE) devices and PE routers. This configuration allows for the extension of routing reachability across a service provider backbone without exposing the internal routing infrastructure. In these designs, BGP carries not only IPv4 and IPv6 reachability but also VPNv4 or VPNv6 routes, enabling the support of multiple virtual routing and forwarding instances across the same physical infrastructure. GRE provides the encapsulation needed to keep these sessions logically isolated, and BGP manages the policy, filtering, and propagation of routes within the VPN.

When configuring BGP over GRE, each endpoint must first ensure that the GRE tunnel is established and that the endpoints are reachable through the underlying IP network. Once the tunnel is operational, BGP peerings are defined using the tunnel interface IPs as the local and remote addresses. The session is then established as if the two routers were directly connected. Depending on the design, this could involve internal BGP (iBGP) or external BGP (eBGP), with different behaviors in terms of route propagation, AS path manipulation, and next-hop processing. The use of loopback interfaces as the BGP source can improve reliability and ensure that the session remains active even if one of the physical interfaces goes down, as long as the GRE tunnel remains reachable.

Route selection and policy control are essential components of BGP, and when used over GRE, these capabilities become even more powerful. BGP policies can be applied to selectively advertise or suppress routes over the GRE tunnel, enforce path preferences, or control outbound traffic flow based on community attributes or local preference values. The GRE tunnel itself can be assigned a higher or lower metric using routing policies or route-maps, allowing it to be used as a primary or backup path depending on network conditions. BGP's support for multiple paths and route reflectors enables complex designs where GRE tunnels serve as overlay links for interconnecting various routing domains in a controlled and scalable way.

Resilience and redundancy are also enhanced by the integration of BGP with GRE. In designs with multiple GRE tunnels between the same two sites or among a group of sites, BGP can be configured to use multiple paths or fail over automatically in case of tunnel failure. This provides not only high availability but also enables load balancing across multiple tunnels, improving bandwidth utilization and network performance. When combined with features such as BFD (Bidirectional Forwarding Detection), GRE tunnel failures can be detected rapidly, and BGP sessions can be reset or rerouted accordingly, minimizing downtime.

Security remains a key consideration in GRE with BGP deployments. Since GRE does not provide encryption or authentication, the BGP sessions and any data carried over the tunnel can be vulnerable if traversing untrusted networks. To protect the integrity and confidentiality of the routing sessions, IPsec is often employed in conjunction with GRE. IPsec encrypts the GRE packets and ensures that they are delivered securely between endpoints. This is especially important in scenarios where BGP is being used to exchange sensitive routing information or where the GRE tunnel crosses the public internet. By combining GRE's encapsulation capabilities with IPsec's encryption and BGP's route management, organizations can build secure, scalable, and policy-driven network architectures.

Monitoring and troubleshooting are critical in any BGP deployment, and GRE adds an additional layer that must be accounted for. Tools such as traceroute, ping, and interface statistics can help verify the status of the GRE tunnel and the BGP session. Logging and SNMP traps can be used to detect when BGP peerings go down or when tunnels become unreachable. It is important to ensure that the GRE tunnel's MTU is properly configured to avoid fragmentation, particularly when IPsec is also in use. Misconfigurations at the GRE or BGP level can lead to routing loops, black holes, or asymmetric routing, so thorough validation and testing are essential during deployment.

GRE with BGP integration enables a wide range of networking scenarios, from enterprise WAN overlays and secure remote peering to large-scale service provider designs and cloud hybrid architectures. It allows routing domains to be extended logically over arbitrary physical paths, simplifies the interconnection of autonomous systems, and provides the tools needed to manage complex routing policies and traffic flows. Through the combined capabilities of encapsulation, encryption, and dynamic routing, GRE with BGP forms a critical foundation for modern IP networks that require flexibility, control, and security.

GRE over IPv6 Networks

Deploying GRE over IPv6 networks represents an important evolution in tunneling technologies, particularly as the global shift from IPv4 to IPv6 continues. GRE, or Generic Routing Encapsulation, has long been used to encapsulate a variety of Layer 3 protocols, including multicast, broadcast, and even non-IP protocols, inside an IP packet. Traditionally, GRE tunnels have used IPv4 as their transport layer, but as IPv6 adoption increases and IPv6-only environments become more common, support for GRE over IPv6 has become essential. This configuration allows the encapsulation of IPv4, IPv6, or other protocol packets within an IPv6 outer header, enabling organizations to extend legacy services, build overlay networks, and maintain compatibility across dual-stack and IPv6-only infrastructures.

Configuring GRE over IPv6 begins with the establishment of a tunnel between two routers that each have an IPv6 address. Unlike traditional GRE, where the source and destination of the tunnel are IPv4 addresses, GRE over IPv6 uses IPv6 addresses for both the tunnel source and tunnel destination. These addresses must be globally routable or reachable through the underlying transport network. Once reachability is confirmed, the GRE tunnel interface can be defined on each router. The tunnel interface is configured with a tunnel mode that explicitly specifies GRE over IPv6, distinguishing it from default GRE or GRE over IPv4 modes. An inner IP address, which may be either IPv4 or IPv6, is then assigned to the tunnel interface to facilitate packet forwarding and routing decisions.

One of the primary motivations for deploying GRE over IPv6 is the need to maintain IPv4-based applications and services while migrating to IPv6 transport. Many enterprises and service providers operate dual-stack networks, where both IPv4 and IPv6 coexist. In such environments, GRE over IPv6 tunnels can be used to connect IPv4 islands across an IPv6-only backbone. This allows legacy systems to continue functioning without requiring immediate upgrades or dual-stack support on every segment of the network. The GRE tunnel encapsulates the IPv4 packets and transmits them across the IPv6 infrastructure, where they are decapsulated and forwarded normally. This provides a seamless mechanism for bridging the protocol gap during transitions and deployments.

GRE over IPv6 also offers benefits in terms of address space and routing efficiency. IPv6 provides a vastly larger address pool, which simplifies the allocation of tunnel endpoints and reduces the likelihood of address conflicts. Additionally, the use of IPv6 as the transport layer can help optimize routing decisions by leveraging IPv6-specific features such as flow labels and improved header compression. In large-scale deployments, where thousands of tunnels may be required, the scalability of IPv6 addressing becomes a significant advantage. It eliminates the need for NAT and allows for direct end-to-end connectivity between GRE tunnel endpoints.

Another advantage of GRE over IPv6 is its compatibility with modern security frameworks and routing protocols. GRE tunnels can be combined with IPsec to secure the encapsulated traffic, ensuring confidentiality and integrity even across untrusted IPv6 networks. This is especially important when deploying GRE tunnels over the public internet or shared service provider backbones. IPsec can be configured in transport mode to secure the GRE packet payload or in tunnel mode to protect the entire GRE-encapsulated packet. When properly configured, this combination provides a flexible and secure method for interconnecting networks that require both encapsulation and encryption.

Dynamic routing protocols such as OSPFv3, EIGRP for IPv6, and BGP can operate effectively over GRE tunnels configured on IPv6 transport. These protocols recognize the GRE tunnel interface as a valid routing path and can establish neighbor adjacencies over it. This enables dynamic exchange of routing information between IPv6 and IPv4 domains, depending on the configuration of the tunnel interface and the routing process. For example, an IPv6 GRE tunnel may be used to transport OSPFv2 packets for IPv4 routing, or to extend an OSPFv3 area across multiple locations using an IPv6 backbone. The flexibility of GRE encapsulation supports these use cases and enhances the interoperability of mixed protocol environments.

Despite its many advantages, deploying GRE over IPv6 does require attention to detail and careful planning. One of the most critical considerations is the correct handling of packet sizes and MTU values. GRE encapsulation introduces additional headers, which increase the total packet size. When transmitted over IPv6 networks, these larger packets may exceed the path MTU, leading to fragmentation or packet drops if not properly managed. Network administrators must ensure that MTU values are adjusted on the tunnel interface and throughout the network path to accommodate the additional overhead. Techniques such as Path MTU Discovery or setting the maximum segment size for TCP connections can help mitigate issues related to fragmentation.

Another factor to consider is the support of GRE over IPv6 in network devices and operating systems. While modern routers and platforms generally support this configuration, older devices or certain firewall implementations may not recognize or handle GRE over IPv6 traffic properly. It is important to verify compatibility and conduct thorough testing before deploying GRE over IPv6 in a production environment. Firewall policies and security appliances must also be configured to allow GRE encapsulated traffic and ensure that IPv6 routing is correctly implemented to support the tunnel endpoints.

Monitoring and managing GRE over IPv6 tunnels involves the same principles as traditional GRE tunnels but must account for the nuances of IPv6 transport. Tools such as ping, traceroute, and interface statistics can help verify tunnel status and diagnose connectivity issues. Logging and SNMP monitoring can be configured to detect tunnel up/down events, packet loss, and performance anomalies. Because IPv6 networks may span different administrative domains or involve complex routing policies, end-to-end visibility and diagnostic tools are essential for maintaining reliability and performance.

GRE over IPv6 is particularly useful in scenarios involving cloud environments and next-generation networks. Many cloud providers offer native IPv6 connectivity and support GRE tunnels for customer interconnects. By deploying GRE over IPv6, organizations can leverage the global reach and addressing capabilities of IPv6 while maintaining compatibility with internal IPv4 networks. This is especially relevant for hybrid cloud models, where private data centers and cloud-based services must interoperate seamlessly. GRE tunnels serve as the glue between these environments, encapsulating traffic as needed and ensuring secure, predictable transport.

As IPv6 adoption accelerates, GRE over IPv6 becomes an increasingly important tool in the network engineer's toolkit. It provides the flexibility to extend legacy services, connect heterogeneous networks, and support advanced routing and security policies across modern infrastructure. The combination of GRE's encapsulation capabilities with the scalability and future-proofing of IPv6 enables network architects to design solutions that are both resilient and adaptable to changing technology landscapes. Through careful design, testing, and operational awareness, GRE over IPv6 can unlock powerful capabilities in environments that demand protocol interoperability, efficient routing, and long-term scalability.

Dual Stack GRE Tunneling

Dual stack GRE tunneling represents a versatile and strategic approach to network design in the context of the ongoing global transition from IPv4 to IPv6. As enterprises and service providers deploy IPv6 to meet the demands of expanding address spaces, there remains a substantial need to maintain compatibility with legacy IPv4 systems and applications. A dual stack network operates with both IPv4 and IPv6 protocol stacks enabled on the same devices and interfaces, allowing the simultaneous processing of both types of traffic. When combined with GRE, or Generic Routing Encapsulation, the dual stack model allows network engineers to encapsulate and transport both IPv4 and IPv6 packets across any IP-based infrastructure, ensuring seamless communication between disparate parts of the network.

At its core, a GRE tunnel creates a virtual point-to-point link that can encapsulate a variety of Layer 3 protocols. With dual stack GRE tunneling, both IPv4 and IPv6 traffic can be encapsulated within a GRE tunnel, regardless of whether the underlying transport is IPv4 or IPv6. The key to implementing this configuration is enabling both protocol stacks on the tunnel interfaces and configuring appropriate tunnel source and destination addresses. Depending on the design, the tunnel may be GRE over IPv4 or GRE over IPv6, but the payloads traveling within the tunnel can be either IPv4 or IPv6, or even a mix of both. This enables incredible flexibility in how traffic is routed across networks, especially in environments where not all devices or paths support both protocol versions natively.

One of the most significant benefits of dual stack GRE tunneling is its ability to bridge protocol islands. For example, a branch office running IPv4-only applications can connect to an IPv6-only data center through a GRE tunnel that encapsulates IPv4 traffic over an IPv6 transport. Conversely, IPv6-enabled applications can communicate across legacy IPv4 backbones by encapsulating IPv6 packets inside GRE over IPv4. This capability is vital in hybrid networks where upgrades to full IPv6 support are ongoing or unevenly implemented. Dual stack GRE tunnels provide a logical overlay that abstracts the underlying transport limitations and delivers uninterrupted connectivity between protocol-diverse segments.

Another key advantage is the support for routing protocol interoperability. GRE supports the transport of multicast traffic, which is required by many dynamic routing protocols to form adjacencies and exchange updates. In a dual stack GRE configuration, protocols such as OSPFv2 for IPv4, OSPFv3 for IPv6, EIGRP for IPv4 and IPv6, or even BGP with dual address families can be run concurrently over the same GRE tunnel. Each routing process operates independently within its protocol family but uses the same logical interface, simplifying configuration and reducing the number of required tunnels. This unified approach not only streamlines network design but also reduces overhead and management complexity.

Configuring a dual stack GRE tunnel begins with establishing IP connectivity between the two tunnel endpoints using either IPv4 or IPv6 as the outer transport. Once the GRE tunnel is established, the tunnel interface is configured with both an IPv4 and an IPv6 address. This dual addressing allows the interface to participate in both IPv4 and IPv6 routing simultaneously. Routing tables and policies can then be defined for each protocol independently, allowing administrators to control which traffic is routed over the GRE tunnel and which uses native transport paths. Access control lists, route-maps, and policy-based routing can further refine the behavior of traffic entering and exiting the tunnel, ensuring alignment with organizational objectives and security policies.

Performance considerations are important in dual stack GRE deployments. GRE adds an encapsulation overhead to each packet, which increases the total packet size and can lead to fragmentation if not properly managed. When dual stack is involved, the additional IP headers for each protocol must be accounted for. Careful adjustment of the maximum transmission unit (MTU) on tunnel and physical interfaces is required to prevent packet loss and maintain throughput. Administrators must also monitor the path MTU between endpoints, particularly when tunneling over the public internet or networks with varying MTU sizes. Tools such as ICMP error messages and path MTU discovery are useful in identifying and resolving related issues.

Security is another critical aspect of dual stack GRE tunneling. Because GRE does not include built-in mechanisms for encryption or authentication, it is vulnerable to interception, spoofing, or denial-of-service attacks if used over untrusted networks. To mitigate these risks, GRE is often deployed in combination with IPsec. IPsec can secure both IPv4 and IPv6 traffic encapsulated in GRE tunnels, providing confidentiality, data integrity, and authentication. This is especially important in dual stack environments where sensitive data or control plane traffic may traverse public networks. Implementing GRE over IPsec in dual stack mode allows organizations to meet stringent security requirements without sacrificing protocol compatibility or flexibility.

Monitoring and troubleshooting are essential to maintaining a stable dual stack GRE deployment. Dual stack introduces complexity in terms of addressing, routing, and protocol behavior, making visibility tools and logging crucial. Network administrators should ensure that they can observe GRE tunnel status, IP reachability, and routing protocol adjacencies for both IPv4 and IPv6. Interface counters, debug messages, and SNMP monitoring can all provide valuable insight into tunnel health and performance. Troubleshooting tools such as ping, traceroute, and packet captures must be used with awareness of the dual stack environment, ensuring that tests are run with the correct protocol version and source addresses.

Dual stack GRE tunneling is especially relevant in large enterprise, service provider, and hybrid cloud scenarios. As more applications and services become IPv6-aware, while many legacy systems remain IPv4-

only, the ability to support both simultaneously becomes a strategic necessity. GRE provides the encapsulation mechanism to carry traffic over any IP-compatible path, and the dual stack model ensures that both generations of the protocol can coexist without disruption. In cloud deployments, GRE tunnels can connect virtual private clouds across regions or between cloud providers and on-premises networks, supporting both IPv4 and IPv6 application traffic. This approach supports business continuity, gradual migration, and seamless interoperability across a wide range of use cases.

Through thoughtful design, proper configuration, and ongoing management, dual stack GRE tunneling enables robust and future-ready network connectivity. It bridges protocol gaps, supports the evolution toward IPv6, and maintains compatibility with critical IPv4 systems. Whether used for dynamic routing, application transport, or secure site-to-site connectivity, this technique delivers a flexible and efficient solution for navigating the dual protocol realities of modern networks. Its role in enabling scalable, interoperable, and secure communication across increasingly complex infrastructures makes it a vital tool in the hands of network architects and engineers worldwide.

GRE in Service Provider Networks

GRE, or Generic Routing Encapsulation, plays a crucial role in service provider networks by enabling flexible, scalable, and protocol-independent tunneling across large-scale infrastructures. Service providers operate in environments that require interconnection of customer sites, delivery of value-added services, and transport of various traffic types across a shared backbone. GRE offers a versatile encapsulation mechanism that supports both unicast and multicast traffic, as well as a wide range of Layer 3 protocols, making it an essential tool in the service provider's operational toolkit. Through GRE, providers can build logical overlay networks that extend customer connectivity across geographically dispersed regions, integrate legacy systems, and support dynamic routing across otherwise incompatible infrastructures.

In a typical service provider architecture, the physical and logical topologies often diverge. The core of the network is optimized for high-speed IP transport, while customer demands require the support of different address families, routing protocols, and topologies. GRE facilitates the abstraction of the core infrastructure from the customer-facing services by creating virtual point-to-point tunnels between provider edge devices. These tunnels allow the provider to deliver IP connectivity between customer sites without exposing or involving the internal routing of the provider backbone. Each GRE tunnel forms a separate overlay that encapsulates the customer's packets, allowing different customers to use overlapping address spaces or custom routing configurations without interference.

GRE's protocol agnosticism is particularly advantageous in service provider contexts. Providers may serve clients who use IPv4, IPv6, or even non-IP protocols such as MPLS or IPX in legacy deployments. GRE can encapsulate any of these protocols and transport them over the provider's IP infrastructure. This allows the service provider to offer flexible and future-proof services that can adapt to changing customer needs and technologies. For instance, an IPv6 customer can be connected through an IPv4 provider network by encapsulating their IPv6 traffic within GRE tunnels. This same mechanism can be reversed to support IPv4 customers over an IPv6 backbone, facilitating the transition to modern protocol stacks without requiring immediate infrastructure overhaul.

Dynamic routing support is another key benefit of GRE in service provider networks. Many customer configurations require the use of dynamic routing protocols such as OSPF, EIGRP, or BGP. These protocols often depend on multicast or broadcast traffic to establish neighbor adjacencies and exchange routing information. GRE supports the encapsulation of multicast packets, which is not possible with simpler tunneling mechanisms like IP-in-IP. This capability allows service providers to extend dynamic routing across their infrastructure transparently. For example, a customer can run OSPF between two geographically separated offices, and the service provider can establish GRE tunnels between the customer edge routers, enabling full OSPF adjacency and route exchange over the service provider's core without any changes to their own routing policies.

Another strategic use of GRE in service provider networks is the implementation of managed VPN services. While MPLS Layer 3 VPNs are often the preferred approach for high-scale environments, GRE-based VPNs provide a simpler and more flexible alternative, especially for smaller customers or in cases where full MPLS infrastructure is not available. In a GRE-based VPN, the provider establishes GRE tunnels between customer sites or between the provider edge and customer edge routers. The tunnels carry encapsulated customer traffic, which can include any Layer 3 protocol, and maintain logical isolation through separate tunnel configurations. These VPNs can be secured by integrating IPsec, providing confidentiality and integrity for the encapsulated data. GRE over IPsec thus becomes a powerful solution for service providers delivering secure site-to-site connectivity without the need for full MPLS deployment.

Service providers also use GRE as a foundation for advanced services such as multicast distribution, traffic engineering, and high-availability architectures. Multicast applications, such as IPTV or real-time data feeds, require reliable transport of multicast packets across the provider's core. GRE tunnels can carry multicast streams from a central source to remote distribution points, even across networks that do not natively support multicast. By encapsulating the multicast packets in GRE, providers ensure consistent delivery regardless of the underlying transport limitations. GRE can also be combined with routing policies and filtering mechanisms to direct specific traffic flows through designated paths, enabling basic forms of traffic engineering.

In high-availability designs, GRE enables redundancy and fast failover through the use of multiple tunnels and routing protocols. Providers can configure primary and secondary GRE tunnels between sites and use dynamic routing to detect tunnel failures and redirect traffic accordingly. With protocols such as BGP or OSPF operating over GRE, changes in tunnel availability can trigger immediate routing updates, minimizing downtime. In combination with monitoring protocols like Bidirectional Forwarding Detection (BFD), GRE-based architectures can achieve sub-second convergence times, ensuring that customer services remain uninterrupted even during infrastructure faults.

GRE's simplicity and broad support across platforms make it particularly attractive to service providers. It is widely supported on routing devices from different vendors and can be configured quickly with minimal complexity. This enables providers to respond rapidly to customer demands, create temporary connectivity for testing or migrations, or deploy bespoke services that would be more difficult to implement using more rigid technologies. The operational overhead is relatively low, and with proper configuration, GRE tunnels can be easily managed, monitored, and integrated into existing network management systems.

Nevertheless, service providers must also address certain limitations when deploying GRE at scale. Because GRE lacks inherent encryption, all traffic within the tunnel is visible unless additional security mechanisms like IPsec are implemented. Furthermore, GRE adds overhead to packets due to its encapsulation headers, which may impact MTU and lead to fragmentation if not carefully accounted for. Providers must plan for this by adjusting MTU settings and using path MTU discovery techniques. Load balancing and quality of service may also be affected if not properly configured, especially in environments with multiple GRE tunnels or complex routing policies.

Despite these considerations, GRE remains a foundational technology in service provider environments. Its flexibility, interoperability, and support for diverse protocols and services allow it to meet a wide range of customer requirements. Whether used for VPN services, multicast delivery, legacy protocol support, or dynamic routing extensions, GRE continues to deliver value in modern service provider architectures. As networks evolve toward increased virtualization, cloud integration, and software-defined paradigms, GRE retains its relevance by providing a reliable and adaptable method for building overlay networks and supporting differentiated services across shared infrastructures. Through thoughtful design and integration, service providers can leverage GRE to enhance their offerings and maintain operational agility in a competitive and constantly changing landscape.

GRE in Enterprise Networks

GRE, or Generic Routing Encapsulation, has established itself as a fundamental technology within enterprise networks, offering a simple yet powerful mechanism for encapsulating Layer 3 packets over IP infrastructure. In the enterprise context, where geographic distribution, protocol diversity, and secure communication are daily operational requirements, GRE becomes a critical tool for constructing scalable, flexible, and protocol-agnostic tunnels between network segments. Its ability to carry multicast, broadcast, and various Layer 3 protocols across IP-based infrastructure makes it especially well-suited for connecting branch offices, supporting legacy applications, and enabling routing protocol continuity across disparate environments.

Within a typical enterprise, networks are often spread across multiple physical locations including headquarters, regional offices, data centers, and cloud-based environments. Despite the shift toward cloud-native applications and centralized resources, local routing decisions, branch connectivity, and secure communications between on-premises segments remain essential. GRE allows enterprises to create logical point-to-point tunnels over existing IP networks, such as the public internet or third-party WAN links, effectively bridging remote sites as if they were on the same local infrastructure. This logical connectivity simplifies route distribution and policy enforcement by enabling enterprise administrators to treat distant sites as part of the same IP topology, regardless of the complexity or limitations of the underlying transport.

One of the primary advantages of using GRE in enterprise networks is its ability to encapsulate various routing protocols, including those that rely on multicast traffic such as OSPF or EIGRP. In many enterprise environments, dynamic routing is used to ensure that routing tables stay up to date as network topologies evolve. However, the underlying transport networks, especially public ones, often do not support multicast traffic. GRE tunnels overcome this limitation by encapsulating multicast packets within unicast IP headers, allowing routing protocols to form neighbor relationships and exchange routes transparently over any IP network. This capability enables enterprises to maintain consistent and automated routing across their entire network footprint, even when connecting locations with different types of infrastructure or service providers.

GRE also plays a significant role in enterprise redundancy and failover strategies. By establishing multiple GRE tunnels between sites, enterprises can implement dynamic routing protocols that detect tunnel failures and reroute traffic through alternate paths without manual intervention. This design supports high availability and improves resilience to link or device failures. Combined with monitoring tools such as Bidirectional Forwarding Detection, GRE tunnel interfaces can be continuously verified, allowing routing protocols to react quickly when a failure occurs. In addition to fault tolerance, GRE tunnels can be configured to support load balancing across multiple paths, enhancing bandwidth utilization and improving performance in bandwidth-constrained environments.

Security is a critical concern in enterprise networks, particularly when traffic traverses untrusted networks such as the public internet. While GRE itself does not provide encryption or authentication, it is often combined with IPsec to secure the encapsulated packets. GRE over IPsec becomes a powerful combination that delivers both encapsulation flexibility and transport security. Enterprises can use this model to create secure site-to-site VPNs, enabling encrypted communication between remote offices while supporting dynamic routing and multicast traffic. This approach is particularly valuable when enterprises need to deploy secure tunnels for voice, video, or internal applications without sacrificing routing capabilities.

GRE also provides value in scenarios involving the migration to IPv6. Many enterprise networks continue to operate predominantly with IPv4, while also preparing for IPv6 adoption. GRE facilitates this transition by enabling IPv6 traffic to be tunneled over an existing IPv4 infrastructure or vice versa. This allows for gradual deployment and testing of IPv6 services without disrupting existing operations. For example, an enterprise may use GRE to connect IPv6-enabled remote branches to a centralized data center over an IPv4-only transport backbone, allowing new IPv6 services to be introduced while maintaining compatibility with the current infrastructure.

In hybrid cloud deployments, GRE offers a flexible method for connecting cloud-hosted resources to on-premises systems. As enterprises increasingly adopt cloud services for scalability and cost efficiency, maintaining secure and consistent connectivity between cloud and on-premises environments becomes a challenge. GRE tunnels can be used to extend the enterprise network into the cloud, allowing applications and services to communicate over a consistent IP topology. When combined with dynamic routing, GRE enables cloud-hosted routers to learn enterprise routes automatically and participate in the overall routing domain. This reduces the need for complex static routing and manual configurations, accelerating deployment and simplifying management.

From a design perspective, GRE is relatively simple to implement and supported by most enterprise-grade routers and firewalls. A GRE tunnel requires only the specification of a tunnel source and destination IP address, along with optional parameters such as keepalives or quality-of-service markings. Once configured, the tunnel interface can be treated like any other IP interface, supporting routing, ACLs, and monitoring. This simplicity allows network engineers to deploy GRE tunnels quickly, test new architectures, and make iterative changes without significant downtime or operational risk.

However, despite its strengths, GRE is not without challenges. The encapsulation process adds overhead to each packet, which can increase the risk of fragmentation if not properly managed. Enterprises must account for this additional overhead by adjusting the maximum transmission unit on tunnel and physical interfaces and ensuring that intermediate devices support the required MTU. Fragmentation can negatively impact performance, especially for latency-sensitive applications such as VoIP or real-time video. Path MTU discovery can help alleviate these concerns, but proper design and consistent policy enforcement across all network elements are essential.

Monitoring GRE tunnels in enterprise networks is vital for maintaining reliability and performance. Administrators should routinely inspect tunnel interfaces, log tunnel events, and use SNMP or other monitoring tools to track tunnel status, throughput, and error rates. Tools such as NetFlow, IP SLA, and packet captures can help diagnose performance bottlenecks or misconfigurations. In complex environments with dozens or hundreds of GRE tunnels, automation and centralized management become critical. Enterprises may leverage network orchestration tools to automate the provisioning and monitoring of tunnels, integrate GRE status into dashboards, and generate alerts when tunnel behavior deviates from expected norms.

GRE has proven itself as a reliable and adaptable solution for enterprise networking challenges. Whether used to extend routing domains, support protocol interoperability, connect remote sites, enable secure VPNs, or bridge hybrid cloud architectures, GRE offers the flexibility and control needed to meet a wide range of enterprise requirements. By encapsulating traffic in a lightweight and transparent manner, GRE empowers enterprises to build robust, resilient, and future-ready networks that can evolve with business needs and technological advancement. Its enduring relevance and widespread support make it a cornerstone of modern enterprise network design.

GRE for Site-to-Site VPNs

GRE for site-to-site VPNs provides a flexible and widely supported solution for connecting geographically dispersed networks securely over untrusted infrastructures such as the public internet. In a site-to-site VPN, the goal is to establish a persistent, reliable, and secure communication path between two or more distinct network locations. While traditional IPsec VPNs are often used to meet the security requirements of these connections, they are limited in certain ways when it comes to encapsulating traffic types or supporting dynamic routing protocols. GRE, or Generic Routing Encapsulation, fills in these gaps by creating a virtual point-to-point link that can encapsulate any Layer 3 protocol, including multicast and broadcast traffic, which are essential for routing protocol exchanges. When combined with IPsec, GRE enables the creation of site-to-site VPNs that are not only secure but also operationally robust and protocol-independent.

The primary benefit of using GRE for site-to-site VPNs is its ability to encapsulate a wide range of protocols. Unlike pure IPsec, which primarily secures unicast IP packets, GRE can carry multicast traffic and non-IP protocols such as IPX or AppleTalk. This makes GRE especially valuable in networks where routing protocols like OSPF, EIGRP, or even RIP need to operate across the VPN tunnel. These protocols typically rely on multicast or broadcast mechanisms to form neighbor relationships and exchange routing information, capabilities that GRE natively supports. By encapsulating such traffic inside GRE and then securing it with IPsec, enterprises can extend their dynamic routing infrastructure across multiple sites without sacrificing security or requiring extensive reconfiguration of protocol behavior.

Configuring a GRE-based site-to-site VPN typically involves defining a GRE tunnel between the edge routers of two locations. Each router must have a public-facing interface with an IP address reachable by the other, and these IP addresses become the source and destination of the GRE tunnel. A virtual tunnel interface is created on each device and configured with an internal IP address that belongs to a common subnet shared across the tunnel. This tunnel interface then serves as the gateway for traffic destined for the remote network. Once the tunnel is up, routing protocols can be activated on the tunnel interfaces to dynamically exchange routes. Alternatively, static routes can be configured for more controlled environments.

To ensure the confidentiality, integrity, and authenticity of the traffic traversing the GRE tunnel, IPsec is applied. IPsec is not aware of the specific contents of the GRE packet; it simply treats the entire GRE packet, including its IP header and payload, as data to be encrypted. This separation of roles allows each protocol to do what it does best— GRE handles encapsulation and protocol support, while IPsec ensures secure transport. IPsec can operate in either transport mode or tunnel mode, though in most site-to-site VPN implementations, tunnel mode is preferred for its simplicity and compatibility. When configured in tunnel mode, the original GRE-encapsulated packet is further wrapped in an IPsec header and transmitted across the internet, ensuring that the contents of the VPN are shielded from inspection or tampering.

GRE for site-to-site VPNs is highly adaptable and scales well in hub-and-spoke topologies. In such designs, a central hub router maintains GRE tunnels with multiple spoke routers at branch sites. Each spoke site uses its GRE tunnel to reach the hub, and the hub routes traffic between spokes as necessary. This model centralizes management and simplifies policy enforcement but can create a single point of failure. To improve resilience, redundancy can be introduced by establishing backup GRE tunnels, using dynamic routing protocols to detect failures, and rerouting traffic automatically. When properly configured, this architecture enables seamless failover and robust site-to-site communication, ensuring business continuity even during partial outages.

Performance considerations are important when deploying GRE-based VPNs. The encapsulation introduced by GRE adds an additional header, typically 24 bytes in size, which can push packets over the maximum transmission unit of the underlying physical interface. When IPsec is added to the stack, further overhead is introduced due to encryption headers and trailers. This can lead to fragmentation unless the MTU on the tunnel interfaces is adjusted accordingly. Careful planning and testing are required to determine the appropriate MTU settings, and techniques such as path MTU discovery should be employed to optimize throughput and prevent fragmentation-related issues.

Another operational concern is the visibility and troubleshooting of GRE tunnels in a VPN environment. Because GRE and IPsec operate at different layers, issues can arise in either encapsulation or encryption. Administrators need to monitor tunnel status, interface counters, and routing adjacencies to ensure optimal performance. Logging and diagnostic tools such as packet capture, traceroute, and tunnel-specific debug commands are essential for identifying problems and verifying correct operation. Effective monitoring also includes integrating GRE tunnel metrics into centralized network management systems to alert on tunnel drops, packet loss, or unexpected route changes.

GRE-based VPNs also offer advantages in terms of flexibility and vendor interoperability. GRE is widely supported across most enterprise-grade routers and firewalls, regardless of vendor, making it an ideal choice for heterogeneous environments. Its simplicity of configuration and protocol neutrality allow enterprises to use it in various scenarios, from traditional branch connectivity to temporary migrations and disaster recovery solutions. Furthermore, GRE tunnels can be programmatically managed using automation tools, which is particularly beneficial in environments where rapid provisioning and teardown of VPNs are required, such as in dynamic multi-cloud architectures or during system failover testing.

One particularly useful application of GRE in site-to-site VPNs is in the context of dual stack networks. Enterprises transitioning from IPv4 to IPv6 can use GRE to carry IPv6 traffic over existing IPv4 internet connections or vice versa. This facilitates a smoother transition and enables parallel operation of both protocol families without disrupting existing services. GRE encapsulation hides the internal protocol from the intermediate network, allowing both IPv4 and IPv6 payloads to be securely transported regardless of the native protocol support in the underlying network.

GRE for site-to-site VPNs empowers enterprises to build secure, scalable, and protocol-flexible connections between their remote locations. By combining the encapsulation strengths of GRE with the encryption capabilities of IPsec, organizations gain a tunneling solution that supports dynamic routing, legacy protocol transport, multicast, and secure communication across virtually any IP network. This architecture offers the adaptability to meet a wide range of connectivity needs, whether for global office interconnection, multi-cloud integration, or secure hybrid environments. As enterprise networks continue to grow in complexity and reach, GRE remains a vital tool for achieving reliable and secure site-to-site communication.

GRE for Hub-and-Spoke Topologies

GRE is a key enabler for hub-and-spoke topologies in enterprise and service provider networks, offering a reliable and flexible tunneling mechanism that allows multiple remote locations to communicate with a central site over a shared infrastructure. In this model, a central router known as the hub acts as the focal point for all traffic, while each remote location, or spoke, establishes a tunnel to the hub. This structure simplifies routing, policy enforcement, and management by centralizing control at the hub while enabling scalable expansion as new spoke sites are added. GRE, or Generic Routing Encapsulation, enhances this architecture by allowing the transport of various network layer protocols, including multicast, broadcast, and even routing protocol traffic, which is essential for dynamic connectivity and centralized routing control.

In a typical GRE-based hub-and-spoke configuration, each spoke device is configured with a GRE tunnel that terminates at the hub router. These tunnels are logically point-to-point, and the hub maintains a separate tunnel for each spoke. The hub, therefore, acts as the intermediary for all communication between spokes. If one spoke needs to communicate with another, the traffic is first routed to the hub, which then forwards it to the appropriate spoke. While this indirect routing may introduce some latency compared to full mesh configurations, it dramatically reduces complexity, as the number of tunnels required is proportional to the number of spokes rather than the square of the number of sites. This makes hub-and-spoke topologies more manageable and scalable in larger networks.

One of the main benefits of using GRE in this architecture is its support for dynamic routing protocols. Because GRE tunnels can carry multicast traffic, protocols such as OSPF and EIGRP can be used to dynamically exchange routes between the hub and spokes. The hub serves as the central routing point, learning all routes from each spoke and redistributing them as needed. This centralization allows for consistent routing policies and simplifies route filtering, summarization, and redistribution strategies. Each spoke only needs to establish a neighbor relationship with the hub, rather than forming peerings with every other spoke, which reduces protocol overhead and convergence time.

Another advantage of GRE in hub-and-spoke topologies is its transparency to the underlying network. GRE tunnels encapsulate the original IP packets within new IP headers, allowing them to traverse any IP network, including public internet or MPLS backbones, without concern for the original protocol. This encapsulation ensures that internal addressing, routing policies, or even entire routing domains can be transported across third-party infrastructures without being exposed or affected by intermediate networks. Enterprises benefit from this abstraction, as they can maintain consistent internal IP schemas and routing designs while leveraging cost-effective WAN links or internet-based transport.

Security is often a consideration in hub-and-spoke designs, especially when tunnels traverse untrusted networks. GRE itself does not provide encryption or authentication, but when combined with IPsec, it becomes a powerful and secure tunneling solution. In GRE over IPsec implementations, each GRE tunnel is protected by an IPsec session that encrypts the entire GRE packet. This approach maintains the flexibility of GRE—such as support for multicast routing protocols—while ensuring that the encapsulated data is protected against eavesdropping and tampering. When implemented correctly, GRE over IPsec allows organizations to build secure, centralized, and scalable VPN infrastructures that adhere to modern security standards without sacrificing routing functionality.

Scalability is another critical factor in hub-and-spoke networks. As new remote locations are added, new GRE tunnels are configured between each spoke and the hub. This linear scalability allows network growth without exponential complexity, unlike full mesh topologies that require additional tunnels between each pair of new sites. Centralized policy management at the hub further simplifies the onboarding of new sites. Routing, access control, and quality of service can be configured once at the hub and applied consistently to all spokes. This consistency enhances security, reduces configuration errors, and accelerates deployment time for new remote offices or cloud edge locations.

Performance considerations must also be addressed in GRE hub-and-spoke implementations. Because all traffic between spokes is routed through the hub, the hub must be capable of handling potentially large volumes of traffic. High-performance hardware, redundant links, and load-sharing mechanisms are often necessary at the hub to prevent it from becoming a bottleneck. Additionally, GRE introduces encapsulation overhead, which increases packet size. This can lead to fragmentation if MTU settings are not carefully configured. Administrators must adjust interface MTUs and account for both GRE and optional IPsec headers to prevent performance degradation, especially for latency-sensitive applications such as voice or video.

Redundancy and high availability can be enhanced in GRE hub-and-spoke designs by deploying dual hub routers and configuring failover mechanisms. Each spoke can establish tunnels to both hubs, and dynamic routing protocols can manage the preferred path based on metrics or availability. In the event of a failure at the primary hub, routing protocols detect the failure and redirect traffic through the secondary hub, ensuring continued connectivity. Such designs enhance the reliability of the overall topology and are particularly valuable for mission-critical enterprise networks where downtime is unacceptable.

From a management perspective, GRE simplifies monitoring and diagnostics. Tunnel interfaces on both hub and spoke devices can be monitored for status, traffic, and errors. Standard tools such as ping and traceroute can be used to test connectivity across GRE tunnels. SNMP and network management platforms can be integrated to provide real-time tunnel health monitoring, performance metrics, and alerting. Logging and syslog configurations can capture tunnel up/down events, which is valuable for auditing and troubleshooting. These capabilities provide network administrators with clear visibility into tunnel behavior and facilitate proactive management of the GRE infrastructure.

GRE in hub-and-spoke topologies is also adaptable to hybrid networking models that include cloud-based resources. Many enterprises are extending their private networks into public cloud environments such as AWS, Azure, or Google Cloud. GRE tunnels can be used to connect cloud routers or virtual appliances to the enterprise hub, making the cloud environment an extension of the internal network. With dynamic routing enabled, the cloud site can automatically learn routes to all on-premises locations, and vice versa. This integration supports secure application deployment, hybrid service delivery, and centralized routing control across both physical and virtual infrastructures.

By leveraging the flexibility, protocol independence, and scalability of GRE, enterprises can build hub-and-spoke networks that support dynamic growth, secure communications, and centralized control. GRE's ability to encapsulate diverse traffic types, enable dynamic routing, and integrate with encryption protocols positions it as a foundational technology for modern WAN architectures. Whether connecting branch offices, data centers, or cloud environments, GRE provides the logical framework necessary to unify and simplify distributed networks through an efficient and resilient hub-and-spoke model.

GRE for Full Mesh Topologies

GRE for full mesh topologies enables direct, dynamic, and protocol-transparent communication between multiple network sites without relying on a central hub for forwarding traffic. In a full mesh configuration, every site is connected to every other site through a dedicated GRE tunnel, allowing traffic to flow directly between any two endpoints without intermediate routing. This model enhances routing efficiency, reduces latency, and eliminates potential bottlenecks associated with hub-and-spoke designs. Although it requires more configuration and management due to the increased number of tunnels, a full mesh topology using GRE can provide superior performance and resilience in enterprise, service provider, or hybrid network environments.

The use of GRE, or Generic Routing Encapsulation, in full mesh topologies leverages its ability to encapsulate a wide variety of Layer 3 protocols and support multicast and broadcast traffic. This makes it an ideal tunneling solution when dynamic routing protocols need to be extended across a complex network. GRE allows the creation of point-to-point tunnels between all participating routers, with each tunnel serving as a direct logical path between a pair of locations. These tunnels are treated by the routing process as regular interfaces, and dynamic routing protocols such as OSPF, EIGRP, or BGP can form neighbor relationships across them. This setup facilitates rapid convergence, optimal routing paths, and a decentralized model that avoids single points of failure.

A critical factor in deploying GRE for full mesh topologies is understanding the scaling behavior. The number of GRE tunnels required in a full mesh grows exponentially with the number of nodes, following the formula $n(n-1)/2$, where n is the number of routers or sites. For example, a network with five sites will require ten GRE tunnels, while one with ten sites will need forty-five. As the number of sites increases, the administrative and processing overhead becomes significant. Each router must maintain multiple tunnel interfaces, routing adjacencies, and interface states. This increases the memory and CPU utilization on devices and requires careful planning to ensure network devices are capable of supporting the required scale.

Despite the scaling challenges, the benefits of full mesh GRE topologies are substantial in environments that demand high availability and low latency. Because each site has a direct path to every other site, traffic does not need to traverse intermediate nodes, which reduces round-trip time and minimizes the number of hops. This is especially valuable for latency-sensitive applications such as voice over IP, video conferencing, or transactional systems. In scenarios where the hub in a hub-and-spoke design might become congested or fail, a full mesh topology ensures that no single device becomes a critical failure point, significantly improving the fault tolerance and robustness of the network.

Dynamic routing plays an essential role in managing the complexity of full mesh GRE networks. Protocols like EIGRP and OSPF can automatically calculate the best path between sites and adapt to topology changes without manual intervention. EIGRP is particularly well suited for full mesh GRE deployments because of its efficient neighbor discovery, route summarization, and support for unequal-cost load balancing. OSPF can also be used effectively, though care must be taken to manage areas and prevent excessive link-state advertisement flooding. BGP, while more complex to configure, provides fine-grained policy control and is often used in larger networks that cross administrative boundaries.

Security considerations must also be addressed when using GRE in full mesh topologies, especially when tunnels traverse untrusted networks such as the internet. GRE itself does not offer encryption or authentication, making it vulnerable to spoofing or packet interception. To mitigate these risks, GRE is commonly paired with IPsec, which secures the GRE tunnels by encrypting the encapsulated traffic. When GRE over IPsec is implemented, each point-to-point GRE tunnel is protected by an IPsec security association, ensuring confidentiality, integrity, and authenticity of the data. This configuration allows organizations to maintain the flexibility of GRE while adhering to stringent security policies and compliance requirements.

Another consideration in full mesh GRE networks is the impact of encapsulation overhead. GRE adds extra headers to each packet, which increases the overall packet size. This can lead to fragmentation if the underlying physical interfaces are not configured with appropriate MTU values. Fragmentation can degrade performance and introduce latency, especially for real-time applications. To prevent this, administrators must adjust MTU and maximum segment size settings on GRE tunnel interfaces and ensure that intermediate devices support the encapsulated packet sizes. Path MTU discovery should also be enabled to dynamically adjust to changing network conditions.

Full mesh GRE topologies can also be extended into virtual and cloud environments. In hybrid networks that span on-premises data centers and cloud providers, GRE tunnels can be used to connect virtual routers, cloud-based workloads, and remote offices into a cohesive full mesh architecture. Cloud platforms such as AWS, Azure, and Google Cloud support GRE tunnels either natively or through virtual appliances, enabling direct communication between cloud regions or between cloud and on-premises networks. This model supports distributed applications, dynamic workloads, and real-time data synchronization without relying on centralized connectivity models.

Despite the added complexity, full mesh GRE networks can be efficiently managed with modern automation and orchestration tools. Configuration templates, scripting, and centralized network controllers can simplify the provisioning and maintenance of tunnels, routing configurations, and security policies. Monitoring platforms can provide visibility into tunnel status, routing behavior, and traffic patterns, allowing administrators to quickly detect and respond to anomalies. Integration with network analytics and telemetry systems further enhances operational efficiency by enabling proactive management and capacity planning.

GRE for full mesh topologies is particularly advantageous in organizations that require equal communication priority among all sites, such as multinational enterprises, collaborative research institutions, or federated government agencies. It supports equal access, avoids traffic bottlenecks, and enables site independence, meaning that any site can serve as a communication hub if needed. This is useful in disaster recovery scenarios where regional outages must be mitigated by shifting traffic to unaffected sites without reengineering the entire network.

By leveraging GRE in full mesh configurations, network architects can build robust, low-latency, and resilient infrastructures that support a wide range of applications and services. The flexibility to encapsulate any Layer 3 protocol, support dynamic routing, and secure traffic with IPsec makes GRE an ideal tunneling solution for advanced full mesh deployments. While it demands careful design, resource planning, and ongoing management, the performance and fault tolerance benefits make it a compelling option for high-demand networking environments.

GRE with Recursive Routing Challenges

GRE with recursive routing challenges presents a complex but important topic in advanced network design. While GRE tunnels offer flexibility and protocol transparency for creating virtual point-to-point links across IP networks, they also introduce scenarios where routing loops or unreachable tunnel endpoints can occur due to misconfigured or improperly ordered routing logic. Recursive routing in the context of GRE tunnels refers to a situation where the route to reach the tunnel destination is learned through the tunnel itself. This creates a paradox, where the tunnel cannot come up because the route to its endpoint depends on the tunnel being active, leading to instability, flapping, or total communication failure.

To understand the implications of recursive routing with GRE, it is important to consider how routing tables are constructed and how GRE tunnels are resolved. A GRE tunnel interface requires a defined source and destination IP address. These addresses typically reside on physical interfaces or loopbacks and are used to establish the outer IP header that encapsulates GRE traffic. For the tunnel to function correctly, the router must be able to reach the tunnel destination using its routing table before the tunnel interface can become operational. This route must be valid, static, or dynamically learned through a process that does not rely on the tunnel interface itself. When the only available route to the tunnel destination is learned through the tunnel interface, a recursive dependency is created. The system attempts to use the tunnel to reach the tunnel, resulting in a loop that cannot resolve itself.

This situation often arises in dynamic routing environments where the tunnel is part of a routing domain that redistributes or advertises routes, including those used to reach other tunnel endpoints. For example, if a dynamic routing protocol such as OSPF or EIGRP advertises a route to the tunnel destination through the tunnel itself, the router may mistakenly believe it can reach the tunnel endpoint over the tunnel. When this occurs, the tunnel interface attempts to forward packets to a next-hop that it can only reach if the tunnel is already up, leading to recursive lookups that fail and prevent the tunnel from establishing. In severe cases, this can cause routing instability, route flapping, or even CPU exhaustion due to constant re-evaluation of recursive paths.

One common manifestation of this issue occurs when the GRE tunnel is configured using a loopback interface as the tunnel source. While using loopbacks for tunnel sources is a best practice because of their stability and independence from physical link states, it also requires that the loopback address be reachable via a stable, non-tunneled route. If the route to the remote tunnel endpoint loopback is only available after routing has converged over the GRE tunnel, recursive routing problems will arise. Routers will attempt to send traffic through a tunnel that does not yet have a valid path to its destination, causing the tunnel to remain in a down state or to oscillate between up and down states as routes appear and disappear.

Addressing recursive routing challenges requires careful routing design and route filtering. One of the most effective solutions is to create static routes for the GRE tunnel destination that point to the physical next-hop IP address or interface, bypassing the routing protocol entirely for that specific destination. By doing this, the router always knows how to reach the tunnel endpoint through a physical path, ensuring that the GRE tunnel can come up independently of the dynamic routing protocol. These static routes act as anchor points, breaking the recursive loop and stabilizing the GRE tunnel.

Another approach is to use route maps or distribute lists in dynamic routing protocols to prevent the advertisement or acceptance of routes that would cause recursive dependencies. For instance, filtering the tunnel destination address from being learned via the GRE tunnel interface ensures that the router will not mistakenly believe it must use the tunnel to reach the tunnel. This method is particularly useful in large-scale deployments with multiple tunnels and dynamic route redistribution, where static routing alone may become cumbersome or insufficiently granular.

Administrative distance manipulation is another technique used to control route selection in the presence of recursive routing risks. By ensuring that static or connected routes to the tunnel endpoint have a lower administrative distance than dynamically learned routes, the router prioritizes these paths and avoids resolving the tunnel destination through less-preferable routes that may depend on the tunnel itself. This method works well in environments where hybrid routing is used, such as static routes for critical infrastructure and dynamic protocols for general reachability.

GRE with recursive routing challenges becomes even more pronounced in redundant or multi-path environments where multiple GRE tunnels exist between routers, each potentially learning routes from the others. Without strict controls, routers can create routing loops by sending encapsulated traffic through tunnels that depend on each other for reachability. Careful path selection, route filtering, and the use of tunnel keepalives or Bidirectional Forwarding Detection can help detect and recover from these situations quickly, but the underlying design must prevent such recursive relationships from forming in the first place.

Troubleshooting recursive routing requires detailed visibility into the routing table, tunnel configurations, and route advertisements. Tools such as traceroute, debug IP routing, and interface status commands can provide insight into how the router is resolving the tunnel destination and whether a recursive loop is occurring. Logs and route lookup diagnostics are especially valuable for identifying whether a tunnel's endpoint is being resolved through a tunnel interface, which is the clearest indicator of a recursive routing issue.

Ultimately, the key to avoiding GRE recursive routing issues lies in the separation of control and data planes. Routing information used to bring up the tunnel must not rely on the tunnel itself. This fundamental principle should guide both static and dynamic routing configuration and influence how GRE tunnels are integrated into broader network architectures. Whether used in enterprise, service provider, or hybrid cloud environments, GRE must be deployed with careful planning around route resolution to ensure stability, reliability, and optimal performance across the network.

GRE and MTU Considerations

GRE and MTU considerations are crucial aspects of designing and deploying stable and high-performing GRE tunnels across IP networks. GRE, or Generic Routing Encapsulation, is a widely used tunneling protocol that allows the encapsulation of a wide variety of network layer protocols within IP. It enables the creation of logical point-to-point links over any IP infrastructure and is particularly valued for its flexibility and support for multicast and routing protocol traffic. However, because GRE adds additional headers to every packet it encapsulates, it increases the overall packet size, and this has direct implications for the maximum transmission unit, or MTU, of the path between the GRE endpoints. When MTU is not properly accounted for, packet fragmentation, loss, or performance degradation can occur, leading to poor user experiences, application failures, or routing instability.

Understanding the relationship between GRE and MTU begins with recognizing that every GRE-encapsulated packet includes an additional IP header and a GRE header. The outer IP header is typically 20 bytes for IPv4 and 40 bytes for IPv6, while the GRE header itself is generally 4 bytes, though it can grow larger if options like checksums or keys are used. This means that every GRE packet is larger than the original payload by at least 24 bytes, and in many real-world configurations, this overhead can reach or exceed 40 bytes. If the physical interface transmitting the GRE packet has an MTU of 1500 bytes, which is standard for Ethernet, then any original packet larger than 1476 bytes will exceed the MTU once encapsulated by GRE, resulting in fragmentation unless proactive steps are taken.

Fragmentation is a key concern when dealing with GRE and MTU. If the encapsulated packet exceeds the MTU of the outbound interface, the router must either fragment the packet or drop it, depending on the settings. Fragmentation not only adds processing overhead to the router but also increases the chance of packet loss and reordering, especially in networks where fragmented packets are treated with lower priority or blocked altogether. Fragmented packets can also lead to poor performance for TCP-based applications, which rely on consistent delivery and order of segments. Furthermore, if the original packet has the Don't Fragment (DF) bit set, which is common in TCP/IP communications, and the GRE encapsulated version exceeds the MTU, the router will drop the packet and send an ICMP unreachable message back to the sender. This behavior can disrupt end-to-end connectivity if ICMP messages are filtered or blocked by firewalls along the path.

One method of addressing GRE-related MTU issues is to reduce the MTU on the GRE tunnel interface itself. By lowering the MTU of the tunnel to account for the encapsulation overhead, routers ensure that any packet routed into the tunnel will not exceed the physical interface's MTU once encapsulated. For example, if the physical interface supports a 1500-byte MTU and GRE adds 24 bytes, the tunnel interface MTU can be set to 1476 bytes. This prevents the router from attempting to send packets larger than the path can accommodate, avoiding the need for fragmentation. Adjusting the tunnel MTU is a common best practice in GRE deployments and is often accompanied by tuning the maximum segment size, or MSS, for TCP traffic.

The MSS is the maximum size of a TCP segment that can be sent without fragmentation. Because TCP packets are constructed with the assumption of a certain MTU, reducing the MSS can prevent the generation of oversized packets at the transport layer. MSS adjustment is typically performed on the router or firewall handling the tunnel, which inspects TCP SYN packets and rewrites the MSS value to a lower value that reflects the actual path MTU, minus the GRE overhead. For instance, setting the MSS to 1360 bytes is a common starting point for GRE tunnels over IPsec, where the total overhead can exceed 100 bytes. MSS adjustment ensures that endpoints never generate packets that will require fragmentation once encapsulated, improving application performance and reducing the risk of transmission errors.

Path MTU Discovery (PMTUD) is another technique used to address MTU challenges in GRE networks. PMTUD works by sending packets with the DF bit set and gradually decreasing the packet size until the path can successfully transmit them without fragmentation. When properly configured and allowed to operate unhindered by security devices, PMTUD can dynamically determine the smallest MTU along the path and adjust packet sizes accordingly. However, many networks block ICMP messages, which are essential to PMTUD, rendering it ineffective. For this reason, GRE deployments often rely on static MTU and MSS settings as a more reliable and predictable solution.

In environments where GRE is combined with IPsec, MTU considerations become even more complex. IPsec adds its own set of headers for encryption, authentication, and key management, which can add another 40 to 80 bytes of overhead depending on the algorithms used. When GRE is encapsulated within IPsec, the total overhead can reach 60 to 100 bytes or more. This leaves less room for the original payload and increases the likelihood of fragmentation. Therefore, in GRE over IPsec designs, it is essential to configure both the GRE tunnel MTU and the MSS values carefully, accounting for the total encapsulation stack.

Monitoring and troubleshooting MTU-related issues in GRE tunnels require visibility into interface counters, logs, and diagnostic tools. Interface statistics can reveal high numbers of output drops, fragmentations, or errors that indicate MTU mismatches. Packet capture tools can show where fragmentation occurs or if ICMP unreachable messages are being sent or received. Debugging commands on routers can help trace tunnel behavior and verify whether packets are being dropped due to size constraints. Regular testing using ping with large packet sizes and the DF bit set can also help identify MTU limitations along the path.

GRE and MTU considerations are not only technical necessities but also essential components of maintaining application performance, routing stability, and user experience. By carefully accounting for encapsulation overhead, configuring tunnel interfaces correctly, and implementing MSS clamping and path MTU discovery, network administrators can prevent fragmentation-related problems and ensure that GRE tunnels operate efficiently. As networks become more complex and incorporate hybrid cloud, mobile access, and encryption layers, understanding and managing MTU in GRE environments becomes an even more critical part of modern network design.

GRE with IPsec Encryption

GRE with IPsec encryption is a widely adopted solution for building secure, flexible, and scalable virtual private networks across public or untrusted infrastructures. GRE, or Generic Routing Encapsulation, provides a mechanism to encapsulate a wide range of Layer 3 protocols over IP networks. It allows for the transport of multicast traffic, dynamic routing protocols, and non-IP payloads, which are capabilities that traditional IPsec VPNs alone do not natively support. However, GRE by itself does not provide any security features such as confidentiality, authentication, or integrity. This is where IPsec becomes essential. By combining GRE with IPsec, network administrators can benefit from the rich encapsulation and routing capabilities of GRE while ensuring that all tunneled traffic remains private and secure through encryption and integrity validation.

The integration of GRE and IPsec is conceptually straightforward but operationally significant. GRE is used to encapsulate the original IP packet, adding its own GRE and new IP headers. This encapsulated packet is then passed to the IPsec process, which applies encryption and optionally authentication, wrapping the GRE packet inside an IPsec packet. This process is typically done in tunnel mode, where IPsec encapsulates the entire GRE packet with a new outer IP header, providing both confidentiality and traffic separation from the underlying transport infrastructure. The result is a secure and encapsulated tunnel that supports routing protocols, multicast traffic, and non-IP payloads while ensuring that data cannot be read or modified in transit.

The use of GRE with IPsec is particularly common in enterprise site-to-site VPN deployments, where remote offices need to communicate securely with a central data center or with each other. GRE enables the extension of Layer 3 connectivity across the VPN, supporting the use of OSPF, EIGRP, or BGP between sites. These routing protocols rely on multicast or broadcast traffic to establish and maintain neighbor relationships and exchange route information. Since IPsec alone only supports unicast, routing over IPsec without GRE would require manual configuration of static neighbor definitions, which reduces flexibility and increases administrative overhead. GRE solves this limitation by encapsulating the routing protocol traffic, allowing dynamic routing to operate naturally across the VPN, and IPsec then protects that GRE-encapsulated traffic from interception or tampering.

In practice, configuring GRE with IPsec involves two main steps: setting up the GRE tunnel and applying IPsec protection to the GRE traffic. The GRE tunnel configuration includes defining a tunnel interface, specifying the source and destination IP addresses for the outer IP header, and assigning an IP address to the virtual tunnel interface. This tunnel interface is then used as a routing endpoint for the participating networks. Once the GRE tunnel is operational, IPsec is configured to secure the traffic between the GRE tunnel endpoints. This usually involves defining security policies, specifying encryption and hashing algorithms, establishing a shared key or certificate-based authentication, and creating security associations between the two endpoints. On many platforms, GRE over IPsec is supported as a unified feature, simplifying deployment by automatically applying encryption to GRE traffic using preconfigured profiles or templates.

Performance and overhead are important considerations when using GRE with IPsec. Each encapsulation layer adds headers to the packet, increasing the total packet size and potentially leading to fragmentation if the path MTU is not adjusted accordingly. A typical IP packet of 1500 bytes, when encapsulated in GRE and IPsec, can exceed the MTU of the physical interface, especially when ESP with authentication and encryption is used. To avoid fragmentation and performance degradation, administrators must adjust the maximum transmission unit (MTU) of the tunnel interfaces and use TCP MSS clamping to ensure that applications do not generate packets too large for the encrypted tunnel path. In addition, hardware offloading of encryption and encapsulation can significantly improve throughput and reduce CPU load on the routers or firewalls managing the GRE over IPsec tunnels.

One of the strengths of GRE over IPsec is its versatility in hybrid and multi-cloud environments. Enterprises frequently use GRE over IPsec to connect on-premises data centers to cloud environments or to interconnect workloads across different cloud regions. In such scenarios, GRE provides a consistent and flexible tunneling mechanism that supports dynamic routing, while IPsec ensures that all communications remain encrypted over the public internet. Cloud platforms often support virtual routers or appliances capable of terminating GRE over IPsec tunnels, enabling seamless integration with traditional enterprise networks. This capability allows enterprises to maintain end-to-end routing control and security policies across both physical and virtual infrastructures.

High availability and redundancy can also be implemented effectively with GRE over IPsec. Multiple GRE tunnels can be established between sites, each protected by separate IPsec sessions, providing backup paths in case of link or tunnel failure. Dynamic routing protocols operating over the GRE tunnels will automatically detect failures and reroute traffic to available paths. Additionally, some implementations support failover between GRE over IPsec and other tunneling methods, such as DMVPN or VTI-based tunnels, offering greater design flexibility. Using IPsec in conjunction with GRE also allows granular control over security parameters, including lifetime settings, perfect forward secrecy, and rekey intervals, aligning with organizational compliance requirements and security policies.

Logging and monitoring are essential in GRE over IPsec deployments to ensure tunnel integrity and troubleshoot issues. Monitoring should include tunnel interface status, IPsec security association health, encryption and decryption rates, and error statistics. Many devices support SNMP, NetFlow, or telemetry-based reporting to central monitoring platforms. Event logs can capture tunnel up/down events, rekey events, or authentication failures, providing insight into both operational and security aspects of the tunnel. Diagnostic tools like packet capture and traceroute are helpful in verifying encapsulation and ensuring that the GRE and IPsec layers are functioning as intended.

GRE with IPsec encryption remains one of the most powerful combinations for building secure, dynamic, and protocol-flexible VPN solutions. It bridges the gap between functional connectivity and strong security by allowing complex network protocols to operate over untrusted networks while safeguarding the data in transit. By encapsulating diverse traffic types with GRE and encrypting them with IPsec, network architects gain the ability to create consistent, secure overlays that meet performance, compatibility, and compliance requirements across a broad range of deployment scenarios. Whether in traditional site-to-site VPNs, hybrid cloud integrations, or global enterprise backbones, GRE with IPsec continues to be a cornerstone of secure network design.

Troubleshooting GRE Tunnel Interfaces

Troubleshooting GRE tunnel interfaces requires a detailed understanding of how Generic Routing Encapsulation operates and how it interacts with other elements of the network, such as routing, addressing, interface states, and underlying IP transport. GRE tunnels are used to encapsulate Layer 3 packets and transport them across an IP infrastructure, creating logical point-to-point links between routers that may be separated by multiple intermediate hops or even untrusted public networks. Because GRE tunnels are virtual interfaces that depend on correct configuration and transport-layer reachability, a wide range of issues can prevent them from functioning properly. These issues may manifest as tunnel interface flapping, tunnel status being down, routing protocols failing to form adjacencies, or data not being forwarded through the tunnel. Effective troubleshooting involves methodically verifying configuration, checking IP reachability, monitoring tunnel interface status, and using diagnostic tools to isolate and resolve problems.

The first and most fundamental step in troubleshooting a GRE tunnel is to verify the tunnel's source and destination IP addresses. GRE requires a tunnel source and destination to be explicitly configured, typically as either physical interface IP addresses or loopback addresses. If either of these addresses is incorrect, unreachable, or misconfigured, the tunnel will not establish. A common issue is that the tunnel source IP is tied to an interface that is administratively down or otherwise lacks connectivity to the tunnel destination. Similarly, if the destination IP is incorrect or unreachable due to routing issues or ACLs, the encapsulated packets will never reach the far end. Verifying basic IP connectivity using ping from the tunnel source to the destination is an essential first diagnostic step. If this ping fails, the problem is likely not with GRE itself, but with the underlying network path or routing configuration.

Another common issue arises when the tunnel destination is resolved via a recursive route through the tunnel interface itself. This recursive routing loop can prevent the tunnel from coming up at all, as the router attempts to send packets through a tunnel that depends on itself for reachability. To resolve this, administrators must ensure that the route to the tunnel destination is known via a path independent of the tunnel, typically through a static route or an alternate routing process that does not rely on GRE. Route filtering, administrative distance adjustment, and careful design can all help prevent recursive routing issues, which are a frequent source of tunnel instability and flapping.

Once IP connectivity is confirmed, the next step is to examine the tunnel interface state. Most network operating systems will show a tunnel interface as up or down based on the status of the underlying IP connectivity. If the tunnel interface is administratively up but operationally down, it usually indicates a failure to reach the destination or a mismatch in configuration. Mismatches in tunnel mode, incorrect keepalive settings, or ACLs blocking GRE protocol traffic can all cause the tunnel to fail. Checking the interface status using standard commands will often reveal whether the tunnel is up/down or up/up, and more detailed interface debugging can show packet counts, encapsulation errors, or protocol mismatches.

ACLs and firewall rules are another frequent source of GRE tunnel problems. GRE uses IP protocol number 47, which is distinct from TCP or UDP. Some firewalls and routers block non-standard IP protocols by default. If protocol 47 is being filtered between the tunnel endpoints, the GRE packets will be silently dropped, and the tunnel will never become operational. To confirm this, packet capture tools or firewall logs can be used to check whether GRE packets are being received and processed correctly. Ensuring that both inbound and outbound ACLs permit GRE traffic on intermediate devices is essential for successful tunnel operation.

Troubleshooting routing over GRE tunnels also requires special attention. Once a GRE tunnel is up, routing protocols may still fail to establish adjacencies or propagate routes if there are MTU issues, filtering rules, or neighbor misconfigurations. Many routing protocols rely on multicast traffic to discover neighbors and exchange updates, and GRE allows this multicast traffic to be encapsulated and transported. However, if there are MTU mismatches or fragmentation issues, routing protocol packets may be lost or corrupted, preventing proper neighbor establishment. Verifying that MTU settings on the tunnel interface account for the encapsulation overhead, and adjusting MSS for TCP-based protocols, can resolve many of these issues. Using debug commands specific to the routing protocol in question can help pinpoint whether hello packets are being sent and received and whether neighbors are responding.

Another important troubleshooting step involves checking for GRE encapsulation and decapsulation errors. Routers maintain counters on the tunnel interface that track the number of encapsulated and decapsulated packets. If these counters are not incrementing, or if there are high numbers of errors, it may indicate a problem with how packets are being processed. Causes can include hardware limitations, software bugs, or incorrect configurations such as mismatched tunnel keys. These counters provide valuable insight into whether the tunnel is functioning at the packet level, even if higher-layer protocols are not yet operational.

Keepalive mechanisms can also be used to monitor GRE tunnel health and detect failures. GRE tunnel keepalives work by sending small packets across the tunnel that must be echoed back by the far end. If responses are not received within a defined interval, the tunnel is marked down. While not always enabled by default, GRE keepalives can be a valuable tool in dynamic routing environments to prevent black holes and ensure rapid convergence. Verifying keepalive settings and timers on both ends of the tunnel helps maintain accurate interface status and can prevent routing protocols from relying on dead tunnels.

In cases where GRE is combined with IPsec for encryption, troubleshooting becomes more complex. Both the GRE tunnel and the IPsec session must be established for traffic to flow. A failure in either layer can disrupt communication. IPsec-specific issues, such as mismatched transform sets, missing pre-shared keys, or expired certificates, can prevent encrypted GRE packets from being transmitted or received. Monitoring IPsec security associations, verifying ISAKMP negotiations, and ensuring consistent policy configurations across both ends are necessary steps when GRE is protected by IPsec.

Finally, network administrators should leverage diagnostic tools such as traceroute, ping with the DF bit set, and packet captures to validate the behavior of the GRE tunnel. Traceroute can show the path GRE packets take and whether they are being delivered to the destination. Ping with varying sizes can test for MTU limitations, while packet captures can reveal if GRE headers are present, properly formed, and returned correctly. These tools, combined with systematic verification of configuration and logs, provide a comprehensive approach to diagnosing and resolving GRE tunnel interface problems across a wide range of network scenarios.

GRE Keepalive Mechanism

The GRE keepalive mechanism is an essential component in ensuring the reliability and resilience of GRE tunnels, particularly in scenarios where dynamic routing or failover mechanisms depend on accurate tunnel status. GRE, or Generic Routing Encapsulation, provides a simple and effective way to encapsulate various Layer 3 protocols over IP networks, creating virtual point-to-point links between devices. While GRE itself is stateless and does not include any inherent session-awareness or link monitoring, it can be enhanced with a keepalive mechanism to detect failures and enable responsive network behavior. This feature becomes especially important in larger or more dynamic environments, where incorrect assumptions about tunnel health can lead to routing black holes, stale adjacencies, or unnecessary traffic loss.

A GRE tunnel operates by encapsulating packets in a new IP header with the GRE protocol number and forwarding them to a destination IP address, typically across an IP-based network that may span multiple hops or third-party carriers. However, the nature of this encapsulation means that the tunnel interface can appear to be up even if the remote endpoint is unreachable or the path is broken. From the operating system's perspective, the virtual tunnel interface is bound to a local IP address and a static destination, and unless configured otherwise, its status does not reflect actual reachability. Without a mechanism to verify the liveliness of the remote GRE endpoint, the local router may continue to route packets into a tunnel that is effectively dead, causing data to be silently dropped or misrouted.

To solve this, the GRE keepalive mechanism was introduced. When enabled, GRE keepalives are periodic control packets sent from one end of the tunnel to the other, with the expectation that they will be returned. These keepalives are GRE-encapsulated packets that mimic normal traffic but are specifically formatted to indicate a liveness check. The receiving router decapsulates the packet and sends a response back to the originator. If a predefined number of keepalive replies are missed, the tunnel interface is considered down. The router then updates its interface state, withdraws associated routes, and notifies any dependent routing protocols of the failure. This behavior helps ensure that routing decisions are based on accurate and timely information, enhancing the overall stability of the network.

The GRE keepalive configuration typically involves setting a keepalive interval and a retry count. The interval specifies how often keepalive packets are sent, and the retry count determines how many consecutive keepalives must be missed before declaring the tunnel down. For example, if the interval is set to 10 seconds and the retry count is 3, the tunnel will be marked down after 30 seconds of silence. These parameters can be adjusted to match the desired sensitivity and convergence speed of the network. A more aggressive setting will detect failures more quickly but may be more prone to false positives in networks with intermittent delays or jitter.

It is important to understand that GRE keepalives are unidirectional. By default, only one end of the tunnel sends keepalive packets, and the other simply responds. This means that tunnel health is monitored from one direction only. If bidirectional monitoring is required, the keepalive mechanism must be enabled on both ends of the tunnel. This allows each side to independently verify reachability and react accordingly. In asymmetric routing environments, where traffic may take different paths in each direction, enabling bidirectional keepalives provides a more accurate representation of tunnel health.

GRE keepalive packets must also be treated appropriately by intermediate devices. Because they are encapsulated GRE packets, they use IP protocol number 47 and must be allowed through any firewalls, ACLs, or security appliances in the path. Misconfigured filters can block these packets, causing false tunnel down detections and unnecessary failovers. Network administrators should ensure that devices along the path between tunnel endpoints do not drop GRE protocol traffic and that inspection policies do not interfere with keepalive processing. Packet captures and log analysis can be useful in confirming that keepalives are being transmitted and received as expected.

In dynamic routing scenarios, GRE keepalives play a critical role in maintaining accurate routing information. Protocols such as OSPF or EIGRP often rely on interface status to determine neighbor reachability. When the GRE tunnel interface goes down due to missed keepalives, these routing protocols can immediately withdraw the routes learned over the tunnel and recalculate new paths, minimizing packet loss and convergence time. Without GRE keepalives, the routing protocol may continue to use the tunnel interface until higher-layer timers expire, leading to delays and suboptimal routing. The keepalive mechanism thus acts as a fast failure detection method that bridges the gap between Layer 3 encapsulation and routing protocol responsiveness.

In high availability designs, GRE keepalives are also useful for triggering redundancy mechanisms. Many networks deploy redundant GRE tunnels for failover, load balancing, or geographic diversity. If one tunnel fails and is marked down by the keepalive process, routing protocols or static routing preferences can shift traffic to an alternate tunnel with minimal delay. This design requires careful coordination of keepalive timers, routing metrics, and tunnel priorities to ensure smooth transitions and avoid routing loops or oscillations. Testing failover scenarios in a lab environment can help validate the effectiveness of GRE keepalives in triggering expected behavior under various failure conditions.

While GRE keepalives provide valuable benefits, they do have limitations. They do not measure actual data-plane performance such as latency, jitter, or throughput, and they only test the ability to send and receive control packets. In some cases, data traffic may experience degradation even while keepalives continue to succeed. For more comprehensive monitoring, GRE keepalives can be supplemented with other mechanisms such as Bidirectional Forwarding Detection (BFD), IP SLA probes, or telemetry-based health checks. These tools offer deeper insights into tunnel performance and allow for more nuanced routing decisions based on service-level objectives.

GRE keepalives are a powerful tool for enhancing tunnel reliability, enabling proactive fault detection, and supporting robust routing behavior in complex network environments. By enabling routers to verify tunnel endpoint reachability and take corrective action when needed, they ensure that GRE tunnels remain a dependable foundation for inter-site connectivity, routing protocol transport, and secure encapsulation. Careful configuration, monitoring, and integration with broader network policies allow GRE keepalives to contribute significantly to the resilience and efficiency of modern IP networks.

Performance Impacts of GRE

The performance impacts of GRE are a critical consideration in any network design that incorporates Generic Routing Encapsulation as a method for transporting data across IP-based infrastructures. GRE offers flexibility by enabling the encapsulation of a variety of Layer 3 protocols inside an IP packet, allowing the creation of logical point-to-point connections between devices over a routed backbone. However, the additional encapsulation introduces both bandwidth and processing overhead that can significantly affect network performance, particularly in high-throughput environments, latency-sensitive applications, or resource-constrained devices. Understanding how GRE influences packet size, CPU utilization, throughput, and traffic behavior is essential for network architects and administrators seeking to balance functionality and performance.

One of the most immediate performance impacts of GRE is the increase in packet size due to encapsulation overhead. Each GRE-encapsulated packet includes a new outer IP header and a GRE header, typically adding at least 24 bytes to the original packet. In some configurations, especially those involving optional GRE features such as checksums, keys, or sequence numbers, the overhead can be even greater. If the GRE packet is then further encapsulated with additional layers, such as IPsec for security, the total overhead can exceed 60 to 100 bytes. This additional size may cause packets to exceed the Maximum Transmission Unit of the physical interface, leading to fragmentation unless proactive measures are taken. Fragmented packets consume more bandwidth, require additional processing for reassembly, and are more likely to be dropped by intermediate devices that are not optimized for large or fragmented packets.

To mitigate fragmentation, many network engineers adjust the MTU of the GRE tunnel interface to a value that accommodates the encapsulation overhead. While this prevents packet drops and reassembly delays, it also means that the maximum size of the payload is reduced, potentially limiting the efficiency of high-bandwidth transfers. Applications that depend on large TCP window sizes or require the transmission of large frames may experience reduced throughput over GRE tunnels unless the path is carefully optimized. TCP MSS clamping is often used to control the size of TCP segments sent over the tunnel, ensuring they do not exceed the safe payload size. While this adjustment enhances stability, it can also limit performance in scenarios that would otherwise benefit from larger TCP segments and higher window scaling.

CPU utilization is another key area affected by GRE, especially on software-based routers or firewalls that do not support GRE offloading in hardware. The encapsulation and decapsulation process must be performed for each packet, which can be CPU-intensive on platforms with high packet rates. This is particularly evident in configurations involving high traffic volumes, complex routing, or additional services such as encryption or deep packet inspection. On such devices, GRE processing can quickly become a bottleneck, leading to increased latency, reduced throughput, and even packet loss under load. Network administrators must monitor device CPU usage closely when deploying GRE tunnels, especially in data center or edge environments where performance is critical. In many cases, upgrading to hardware-based platforms with built-in support for GRE offloading can alleviate the performance impact and provide consistent throughput regardless of traffic patterns.

The influence of GRE on Quality of Service (QoS) mechanisms must also be considered. When a packet is encapsulated in GRE, the original Layer 3 header containing QoS markings may be buried beneath the outer IP header. If the intermediate routers and switches are not configured to copy or preserve these QoS markings, the encapsulated packets may be treated as best effort, regardless of their original priority. This can severely degrade the performance of latency-sensitive traffic such as VoIP, video conferencing, or real-time applications. To address this, many platforms allow the configuration of QoS propagation mechanisms that copy the Differentiated Services Code Point (DSCP) or Type of Service (ToS) values from the inner header to the outer header during encapsulation. Proper implementation of this feature ensures that the traffic maintains its intended treatment across the network, preserving performance and ensuring that service-level agreements are met.

GRE also impacts network convergence and routing behavior in scenarios involving dynamic routing protocols. When routing protocols operate over GRE tunnels, any delay or instability in the tunnel can result in slower convergence or route flapping. This may occur if the tunnel interface is marked as up while the remote end is unreachable, a situation that can be partially mitigated by implementing GRE keepalives or Bidirectional Forwarding Detection (BFD). Even with such mechanisms, the encapsulation process introduces additional delay that may affect the responsiveness of the routing protocol, especially in large-scale deployments or real-time failover scenarios. The delay introduced by GRE may not be significant for general web traffic or background applications, but in environments where sub-second failover is required, even small increases in round-trip time can matter.

Another performance consideration relates to multicast traffic, which GRE supports and IPsec does not natively. GRE allows dynamic routing protocols and other multicast-dependent services to operate across tunnel interfaces. While this is an advantage in terms of functionality, multicast traffic can place a higher load on the processing plane, particularly when multiple streams are replicated and forwarded through GRE tunnels. The replication of multicast streams at the source GRE tunnel interface can consume significant resources, especially when the same traffic is destined for multiple tunnel endpoints. This is especially problematic in hub-and-spoke or full mesh topologies where the hub may be required to process and forward the same multicast packets to multiple spokes, multiplying the workload.

GRE's impact on performance can also vary depending on the transport network it traverses. In cases where GRE tunnels are established over public internet paths, variations in latency, jitter, and packet loss may be exacerbated by the encapsulation process. The additional headers increase the chance that packets will be dropped due to MTU mismatches, and encapsulated packets may experience different handling by intermediate devices that do not recognize or optimize for GRE. In managed MPLS environments, where traffic engineering and predictable performance are provided, the impact of GRE is generally less pronounced, though encapsulation overhead must still be considered when sizing circuits and calculating bandwidth utilization.

Ultimately, GRE's performance impact is a combination of the encapsulation overhead, processing load, routing implications, and the behavior of the underlying transport network. While it provides a powerful tool for creating flexible overlays, supporting dynamic routing, and bridging protocol boundaries, GRE must be deployed with careful attention to resource availability, interface configuration, and monitoring. By anticipating the performance costs and implementing optimizations such as MTU tuning, MSS clamping, QoS propagation, and hardware acceleration, network engineers can mitigate the downsides and ensure that GRE tunnels deliver the intended functionality without compromising the stability or efficiency of the network.

Monitoring GRE Tunnels

Monitoring GRE tunnels is an essential task for network administrators seeking to maintain stability, performance, and visibility within complex IP infrastructures. GRE, or Generic Routing Encapsulation, is a powerful tool for encapsulating Layer 3 traffic across routed networks. It enables the creation of logical point-to-point links between geographically dispersed devices and is commonly used in enterprise WANs, cloud interconnects, VPNs, and dynamic routing overlays. However, because GRE tunnels are virtual and rely on underlying IP connectivity, their operational status is not always self-evident. Monitoring GRE tunnels requires more than simply verifying that a tunnel interface is administratively up. It demands a systematic approach to checking tunnel health, traffic flow, encapsulation success, interface performance, and error rates to ensure that data is flowing as expected and that failures are detected early.

The first layer of GRE tunnel monitoring involves interface state observation. Most network devices expose the tunnel interface in the same way they display physical interfaces. These interfaces have operational statuses such as up, down, or administratively down. However, unlike physical links that can detect carrier status, GRE interfaces rely solely on IP connectivity to the tunnel destination. A tunnel can appear to be up even if the remote endpoint is unreachable or if routing issues are preventing packet delivery. This makes it important to monitor both the tunnel interface and the reachability of the tunnel destination. Simple tools such as ICMP ping to the remote GRE endpoint can provide immediate feedback on basic connectivity, but more robust monitoring involves continuous tracking of tunnel state using protocol-specific mechanisms and SNMP-based metrics.

GRE tunnel keepalives are often implemented to provide more accurate state detection. When configured, keepalives periodically send probe packets across the tunnel to confirm the presence of the remote endpoint. If responses are not received within a specified interval, the tunnel interface is marked down. Monitoring the status and results of these keepalives is crucial for understanding whether the tunnel is functionally healthy or simply reporting a logical up state. Logging the loss of keepalives over time can help identify intermittent issues, such as link flaps, upstream congestion, or ACLs blocking GRE protocol packets. Network operators can track the frequency of tunnel resets or transitions from up to down states to build a trend of tunnel reliability and correlate it with upstream network performance.

In addition to monitoring the tunnel interface itself, it is vital to observe traffic counters associated with the GRE tunnel. Most routers and firewalls provide per-interface statistics, including packets sent, packets received, bytes transferred, input errors, output errors, and drops. These counters can be polled using SNMP or collected using streaming telemetry for real-time analysis. A sudden drop in packet throughput or a sharp increase in input errors may indicate encapsulation problems, routing loops, or fragmentation issues due to incorrect MTU settings. Consistently high drop rates on the GRE interface may also suggest CPU congestion, incorrect route redistribution, or a mismatch in tunnel configuration between endpoints.

Packet captures are another valuable tool in GRE tunnel monitoring. Capturing traffic at the physical interface where GRE packets are transmitted or received allows administrators to examine whether the GRE headers are being properly added and removed, and whether payload data is intact. Packet analysis can reveal misconfigured GRE tunnel keys, incorrect source or destination IP addresses, or even outer IP header mismatches that prevent encapsulated traffic from reaching the correct destination. In encrypted GRE deployments, such as GRE over IPsec, packet captures help verify that encapsulated packets are being successfully encrypted, decrypted, and authenticated, adding another layer of assurance for secure communications.

Dynamic routing protocols that operate over GRE tunnels provide another source of tunnel health data. When protocols like OSPF, EIGRP, or BGP are used, their neighbor relationships and routing table entries depend on the tunnel being available and functional. Monitoring the state of routing protocol adjacencies over GRE interfaces gives valuable insight into whether the tunnel is reliably supporting control plane traffic. Flapping neighbor adjacencies or route withdrawal events tied to a specific GRE interface can signal tunnel instability. Event logs and protocol-specific debug commands can pinpoint whether GRE failures are impacting routing convergence and can be correlated with tunnel interface logs to build a clearer diagnostic picture.

Modern network monitoring platforms often include visualization tools that represent GRE tunnels as logical links on topology maps. These tools integrate data from SNMP, syslog, flow exports, and telemetry to provide real-time tunnel performance indicators, including latency, jitter, packet loss, and bandwidth utilization. Such visual dashboards help operations teams quickly identify when GRE tunnels deviate from expected behavior and offer alerts when thresholds are exceeded. Setting performance baselines and configuring alarms for key tunnel metrics ensures that degraded conditions are caught early before they impact applications or users. When tunnels span public or semi-public infrastructure, such monitoring becomes even more critical, as the underlying transport is not under direct control of the organization.

Syslog messages generated by network devices can also provide timely indicators of tunnel events. These messages include tunnel up/down notifications, GRE encapsulation failures, keepalive timeouts, and route changes impacting tunnel paths. Centralized log aggregation platforms can collect and analyze these messages to detect recurring issues or to correlate tunnel instability with scheduled maintenance, DDoS attacks, or upstream outages. Combined with historical tunnel performance data, syslog messages contribute to root cause analysis and long-term optimization efforts.

Proactive monitoring also includes verifying that GRE tunnels are not being used beyond their intended capacity. As bandwidth demands increase due to application growth or traffic redirection, GRE tunnels may become overloaded. Monitoring bandwidth usage trends on tunnel interfaces helps identify when tunnels are approaching saturation and need to be upgraded or load balanced. Traffic shaping and quality of service policies may also need adjustment to ensure that GRE tunnels deliver acceptable performance under varying network conditions. When multiple tunnels exist between sites, performance metrics can guide routing decisions or influence dynamic path selection to maintain optimal performance.

Ultimately, monitoring GRE tunnels is a multi-layered task that involves examining both control and data plane behavior, interpreting interface statistics, analyzing packet flows, tracking dynamic routing behavior, and reacting to event-driven alerts. As networks grow more distributed and complex, especially with the integration of cloud and hybrid environments, the ability to effectively monitor GRE tunnels becomes an essential part of maintaining reliable connectivity. Whether used for dynamic routing overlays, VPN extensions, or protocol encapsulation, GRE tunnels must be continuously observed, measured, and assessed to ensure they deliver the performance, reliability, and functionality expected by the network architecture they support.

GRE with QoS Policies

Generic Routing Encapsulation, commonly known as GRE, is a tunneling protocol that enables the encapsulation of a wide variety of network layer protocols within point-to-point connections. It provides a simple yet powerful mechanism for building virtual point-to-point links over an IP network, which is particularly useful in scenarios such as VPNs, branch-to-branch communication, and legacy protocol transport over IP. However, while GRE offers flexibility and compatibility across different network types, it does not inherently support Quality of Service (QoS) by default. As GRE packets are encapsulated and transmitted through networks, they often lose the QoS markings that were assigned to the original payload, which presents a challenge when consistent service levels and traffic prioritization are required.

To address this, network engineers must carefully implement QoS policies that can coexist and interact effectively with GRE tunnels. The primary objective of integrating QoS with GRE is to preserve or reassign traffic classification and prioritization so that mission-critical traffic can receive appropriate handling across the entire network path. This includes maintaining latency-sensitive traffic such as VoIP or real-time video at the front of transmission queues while relegating lower-priority data like file transfers or updates to best-effort delivery. The key to achieving this is ensuring that QoS markings, such as Differentiated Services Code Point (DSCP) values, are either copied from the original IP header to the outer GRE header or reclassified after decapsulation, depending on the network architecture.

One of the core challenges lies in the encapsulation process itself. When a GRE tunnel encapsulates a packet, a new outer IP header is added, and the original inner header is effectively hidden from intermediate devices that make forwarding decisions based on QoS policies. This means that any DSCP or IP precedence markings in the original packet may no longer influence queueing and scheduling decisions along the network path. To mitigate this, many router implementations offer a feature that copies the DSCP value from the inner IP header to the outer GRE IP header during encapsulation. This ensures that QoS-aware routers and switches between the tunnel endpoints can still apply policies such as Weighted Fair Queuing (WFQ), Class-Based Weighted Fair Queuing (CBWFQ), or Low-Latency Queuing (LLQ) based on the visible markings.

Once the GRE packet reaches the remote tunnel endpoint, decapsulation occurs, stripping off the outer IP and GRE headers to expose the original packet. At this stage, QoS policies can again be applied based on the inner packet's attributes. If the outer header had carried the DSCP value, the remote endpoint can decide to trust this marking or reclassify traffic according to local policy. This flexibility allows administrators to enforce end-to-end QoS, even over transport networks that are unaware of or indifferent to the contents of GRE tunnels. However, such trust should be applied judiciously. If the GRE tunnel traverses an untrusted or third-party network, relying on DSCP values copied into the outer header could introduce risk, as malicious or misconfigured networks might alter these values.

Another layer of complexity appears when multiple traffic classes are multiplexed into a single GRE tunnel. In this case, internal QoS mechanisms must be configured to perform per-class shaping and scheduling before encapsulation. This typically involves using class maps and policy maps to identify and prioritize traffic at the ingress interface, ensuring that voice, video, and data streams are not competing equally for tunnel bandwidth. Traffic shaping plays a crucial role here by regulating the data rate to match the available tunnel capacity, reducing the chance of buffer overflow and packet loss. When implemented correctly, this ensures that time-sensitive traffic maintains consistent performance, even under conditions of network congestion.

Moreover, tunnel bandwidth constraints should be explicitly defined within QoS policies. GRE tunnels are often treated as logical interfaces with no inherent bandwidth limitations. Without defining these constraints, traffic could overwhelm the physical interface, leading to unpredictable behavior. By assigning a bandwidth value to the GRE tunnel interface in the router configuration, the QoS engine is provided with a reference point for allocating resources to different classes of traffic. This bandwidth specification allows for accurate traffic shaping and queue management, aligning with organizational traffic priorities.

One particularly effective method for deploying QoS over GRE tunnels is Hierarchical QoS (HQoS). In this model, a parent policy governs the overall tunnel bandwidth, while child policies manage individual traffic classes within that constraint. This hierarchical structure enables fine-grained control over how bandwidth is distributed and enforces fairness across applications. For example, a parent policy may allocate 10 Mbps to a GRE tunnel, while child policies ensure that 3 Mbps is reserved for voice, 4 Mbps for video, and 3 Mbps for best-effort data. This structured approach enhances predictability and ensures that lower-priority traffic does not starve higher-priority services of necessary resources.

Monitoring and verification are essential components of any GRE QoS deployment. Tools like NetFlow, SNMP, and QoS-specific show commands provide visibility into how policies are applied and how traffic behaves across the tunnel. This operational data is invaluable for troubleshooting and optimization, allowing administrators to fine-tune classifications, verify marking integrity, and adjust bandwidth allocations in response to changing traffic patterns.

Ultimately, integrating GRE with QoS policies transforms what would otherwise be a best-effort tunnel into a deterministic transport path for prioritized services. This capability is crucial in today's enterprise and service provider networks, where application performance and user experience hinge on the reliable delivery of real-time and business-critical data. While GRE itself is simple in design, combining it with robust QoS strategies demands a detailed understanding of encapsulation, marking, classification, and queueing mechanisms. With proper configuration and policy enforcement, GRE tunnels can support sophisticated traffic management schemes, extending QoS guarantees across complex and diverse IP networks.

GRE and MPLS Integration

The integration of Generic Routing Encapsulation (GRE) and Multiprotocol Label Switching (MPLS) has become a vital solution for modern network architectures, particularly in complex enterprise and service provider environments. Both GRE and MPLS offer unique capabilities, and their combination provides enhanced flexibility, scalability, and control over traffic engineering. GRE is primarily used for tunneling traffic across IP networks, encapsulating a wide range of network protocols within a point-to-point virtual link. MPLS, on the other hand, is a powerful data-carrying mechanism that uses labels instead of traditional IP routing to direct packets through a predefined path. When these two technologies are used together, they can bridge the gap between different network domains, support legacy routing protocols, and facilitate traffic segregation and policy enforcement.

One of the most common scenarios for GRE and MPLS integration arises when an organization needs to interconnect routing domains that use overlapping IP address spaces or run incompatible routing protocols. GRE allows the encapsulation of entire routing protocols, such as OSPF or EIGRP, inside tunnels, enabling them to run across an MPLS backbone without interfering with the service provider's internal routing infrastructure. This is especially useful in multi-tenant or multi-vendor environments where routing separation and independence are critical. By encapsulating routing updates within GRE and transmitting them over MPLS Label Switched Paths (LSPs), customers can maintain end-to-end dynamic routing while leveraging the performance and traffic engineering benefits of MPLS.

The encapsulation process in GRE creates a new IP packet with its own header, wrapping the original packet before transmission. When integrated with MPLS, GRE tunnels can serve as payloads that are themselves encapsulated within MPLS labels. This nesting of encapsulations allows for multiple layers of abstraction and control. For example, a GRE tunnel may encapsulate enterprise traffic that is sensitive or requires specific routing policies, while MPLS provides the transport layer, ensuring low-latency, high-availability paths across the provider's network. This dual encapsulation mechanism is particularly effective in scenarios where different sites must be interconnected over a shared backbone without exposing their internal routing details to each other or to the service provider.

Service providers often use MPLS to offer Layer 3 VPN services to customers, and GRE plays an important role in enabling flexible customer connectivity models. In some cases, GRE tunnels are established between customer edge (CE) routers and provider edge (PE) routers, carrying routing information and customer traffic securely over the MPLS network. These GRE tunnels can support multicast traffic, routing protocol adjacency, and non-IP payloads, which are not natively supported by MPLS VPNs. This approach provides a hybrid model where the robustness and simplicity of GRE coexist with the sophisticated label-based forwarding of MPLS, delivering a versatile platform for delivering managed services.

Another compelling reason to integrate GRE with MPLS is to overcome limitations in MPLS deployment, particularly in networks where MPLS cannot be extended all the way to the edge. In such cases, GRE tunnels can bridge non-MPLS-enabled islands to an MPLS core. A branch office with no MPLS capability can establish a GRE tunnel to an MPLS-enabled data center, allowing its traffic to traverse the MPLS network as if it were directly connected. This design allows for incremental MPLS deployment without requiring a complete overhaul of existing infrastructure. It also facilitates the integration of mobile or temporary sites into the MPLS domain, using GRE to establish connectivity while leveraging the performance of the label-switched core.

Traffic engineering is another area where GRE and MPLS integration proves invaluable. MPLS-TE, or MPLS Traffic Engineering, allows the creation of explicit paths through the network, optimizing the use of available resources and ensuring adherence to service-level agreements. When GRE tunnels are used over MPLS-TE LSPs, network operators gain the ability to steer encapsulated traffic along predefined paths, even for traffic that does not support MPLS natively. This is particularly useful for transporting IPv6 or multicast traffic across MPLS cores that were initially designed for IPv4 unicast. By encapsulating such traffic in GRE and transporting it over MPLS-TE, organizations can avoid costly upgrades while extending the life and utility of their existing infrastructure.

Security is also enhanced by the integration of GRE and MPLS. Although neither protocol provides encryption by default, GRE tunnels can be encrypted using IPsec, creating secure tunnels across an MPLS core. This allows sensitive traffic to be protected end-to-end while still benefiting from the efficiency and performance of MPLS transport. Such a setup is especially useful for hybrid cloud architectures and branch connectivity, where encrypted GRE tunnels over MPLS provide a cost-effective and secure alternative to dedicated leased lines or full-mesh VPNs.

Operational simplicity is another benefit that emerges from this integration. Network operators can design flexible and modular architectures where GRE tunnels serve as building blocks for interconnecting various domains, while MPLS ensures optimal path selection and fast reroute capabilities. The administrative separation between GRE tunnel endpoints and the underlying MPLS infrastructure allows for independent troubleshooting, policy enforcement, and scalability. Moreover, with GRE over MPLS, failover scenarios can be handled efficiently by leveraging MPLS Fast Reroute and GRE tunnel redundancy, ensuring high availability and minimal disruption in case of link or node failures.

In practical deployments, integrating GRE with MPLS requires careful planning and configuration. GRE tunnel interfaces must be assigned IP addresses and routing adjacencies must be established over them. The underlying MPLS infrastructure must be capable of transporting the GRE-encapsulated traffic without modifying the payload. In some cases, QoS policies need to be adapted to ensure that the encapsulated traffic retains its priority markings and is treated appropriately throughout the network. GRE keepalives may be used to monitor tunnel health, and routing protocols can be tuned to prefer or failover GRE paths depending on operational requirements.

GRE and MPLS are complementary technologies that, when integrated, offer a powerful toolkit for building flexible, scalable, and secure network topologies. This integration supports a wide range of use cases, from routing protocol transport and multicast delivery to traffic engineering and hybrid cloud connectivity. By combining the encapsulation capabilities of GRE with the performance and intelligence of MPLS, network architects can create adaptable solutions that meet the evolving demands of modern enterprises and service providers.

GRE Tunnels in Cloud Environments

The widespread adoption of cloud computing has significantly transformed how modern networks are designed and operated. As enterprises move their workloads and applications to public and hybrid cloud infrastructures, the need for secure, scalable, and flexible interconnectivity between on-premises environments and cloud platforms becomes increasingly critical. One of the key technologies enabling such connectivity is Generic Routing Encapsulation, or GRE. GRE tunnels offer a method for encapsulating packets in order to traverse different network segments, effectively creating a virtual point-to-point link over an IP-based backbone. In cloud environments, GRE provides a powerful mechanism for extending private networks, supporting dynamic routing protocols, and facilitating the transport of traffic types that are not always natively supported by the cloud provider.

When deploying GRE tunnels in cloud environments, a typical use case involves linking an enterprise data center to a virtual network in a public cloud. While most cloud platforms offer built-in VPN services, these often come with limitations regarding supported protocols, throughput, and feature sets. GRE tunnels, in contrast, can encapsulate a broad range of Layer 3 protocols and even support multicast traffic, which many cloud-native VPN solutions do not allow. This flexibility makes GRE an appealing option for organizations that require the extension of complex routing domains or the continuation of legacy protocol support between on-premises and cloud-hosted infrastructure.

One of the primary advantages of using GRE tunnels in cloud environments is the ability to establish dynamic routing adjacencies across the tunnel. Most cloud providers, including AWS, Microsoft Azure, and Google Cloud, support static routing in their default VPN services, which limits the network's ability to adapt to topology changes or failures. With GRE, it becomes possible to run dynamic routing protocols like OSPF, BGP, or EIGRP between the cloud-hosted virtual router and the enterprise edge router. This dynamic routing capability enables automatic route advertisement, failover, and redistribution, which are essential for maintaining resilient connectivity and consistent network behavior across hybrid environments.

To deploy GRE tunnels in the cloud, organizations typically provision a virtual machine or network appliance that supports GRE encapsulation and acts as a tunnel endpoint. This instance is configured with an external IP address for public reachability and an internal address to integrate into the cloud virtual network. On the on-premises side, a compatible router or firewall is configured to form the other end of the tunnel. The GRE tunnel is established over the public internet or a dedicated private link, allowing encapsulated traffic to traverse securely between both environments. While GRE itself does not provide encryption, it is often combined with IPsec to ensure that data is protected during transit. This combination, known as GRE over IPsec, is particularly popular in scenarios where regulatory compliance and data confidentiality are paramount.

Cloud environments present unique challenges that must be considered when implementing GRE tunnels. One such challenge is the handling of Maximum Transmission Unit, or MTU, size. Because GRE encapsulation adds an additional header to each packet, there is a risk of fragmentation, especially when large packets are transmitted across the tunnel. This can negatively affect performance, particularly for protocols sensitive to latency and retransmission. To address this, MTU sizes must be carefully adjusted on both tunnel endpoints, and Path MTU Discovery should be enabled whenever possible. In some cases, network administrators configure TCP MSS clamping to prevent issues caused by excessive packet sizes.

Another challenge is the cloud provider's network policy restrictions. Some cloud platforms impose limitations on which protocols can be used or how traffic can be routed through their virtual networks. GRE, as a protocol that operates directly over IP without using TCP or UDP, may require special configuration, including the use of security groups, firewall rules, or network security policies that explicitly allow protocol 47, which GRE uses. In addition, cloud platforms may enforce strict anti-spoofing measures or disallow traffic with source IP addresses that do not match the assigned virtual network ranges. These limitations necessitate careful planning and validation during the design and deployment phase.

Despite these challenges, GRE tunnels provide substantial benefits in terms of network flexibility and interoperability. They enable the creation of overlay networks that span across multiple cloud regions and between cloud providers. This is particularly valuable in multi-cloud strategies, where applications and services are distributed across different platforms and require seamless interconnectivity. By using GRE tunnels, organizations can create unified routing domains and consistent IP address schemes, simplifying network management and reducing the complexity of application deployment across clouds.

GRE also plays an important role in supporting advanced networking features in the cloud. For example, multicast applications that require real-time distribution of data to multiple recipients can be supported over GRE tunnels, even if the cloud provider does not natively support multicast routing. Similarly, GRE can be used to transport IPv6 traffic across IPv4-only infrastructures or to carry non-IP traffic between environments. This ability to tunnel a wide variety of traffic types gives organizations the freedom to deploy custom or legacy applications in the cloud without needing to redesign their networking architecture.

In scenarios where multiple customer networks need to be connected to a centralized cloud service, GRE tunnels can provide a scalable solution. Each customer site can establish its own GRE tunnel to a centralized virtual appliance in the cloud, enabling secure and isolated connectivity without requiring the cloud provider to manage individual VPN sessions. This hub-and-spoke model simplifies operations and enables service providers or large enterprises to onboard new sites quickly and efficiently.

GRE tunnels in cloud environments serve as a crucial bridge between the traditional enterprise network and the agile, scalable world of cloud computing. Their flexibility, compatibility with dynamic routing, and support for a wide range of traffic types make them an indispensable tool for network architects. As cloud adoption continues to grow, the role of GRE in hybrid and multi-cloud networking will only become more prominent, enabling organizations to maintain control, visibility, and performance across their increasingly distributed infrastructures.

GRE for Secure Hybrid Deployments

In the evolving landscape of enterprise IT, hybrid deployments have become a foundational model for balancing on-premises infrastructure with the dynamic capabilities of cloud environments. As organizations increasingly adopt a hybrid architecture, the need for secure, reliable, and flexible communication channels between disparate components becomes critical. Generic Routing Encapsulation, or GRE, offers a solution to bridge these separate environments into a cohesive network. GRE provides a mechanism for encapsulating packets from one network protocol within the packets of another, allowing virtually any network layer protocol to be tunneled over an IP infrastructure. This is particularly valuable in hybrid deployments where interoperability, control, and flexibility are paramount.

Secure hybrid deployments often involve the integration of enterprise data centers, remote branch offices, and multiple cloud environments into a single operational ecosystem. Each of these segments may run different network protocols, use dissimilar address spaces, or operate under independent administrative policies. GRE tunnels allow for the abstraction of these differences by creating virtual point-to-point links over existing IP networks. These tunnels serve as dedicated paths through which traffic can securely traverse the public internet or third-party networks without requiring major changes to the underlying infrastructure. GRE tunnels can encapsulate routing protocol updates, multicast traffic, and even legacy protocol communications, making them an adaptable choice for hybrid network designs.

One of the defining characteristics of hybrid deployments is the need for secure data transport. While GRE itself does not include built-in encryption or integrity checking, it is commonly combined with IPsec to form GRE over IPsec tunnels. In this configuration, GRE provides the encapsulation layer, allowing complex or non-IP traffic to be tunneled, while IPsec delivers encryption, authentication, and anti-replay protection. This combination enables secure communication between disparate environments while preserving advanced networking capabilities such as dynamic routing and multicast support. This layered approach is particularly beneficial when branch offices or remote workloads need to access central services hosted either in a data center or a cloud region without compromising security.

The use of GRE in secure hybrid deployments is not limited to data encryption. It also plays a crucial role in maintaining consistent routing and segmentation. With GRE tunnels in place, administrators can extend routing protocols such as OSPF, BGP, or EIGRP across the hybrid environment, allowing for automatic route updates, failover, and policy-based routing. This dynamic routing capability ensures that network paths are always up-to-date, even as cloud instances are scaled up or down, or as network links become unavailable. Furthermore, the use of GRE allows traffic segmentation and isolation, supporting multiple tenant environments or logical divisions within a single organization. Each GRE tunnel can be dedicated to a specific department, application, or customer, providing granular control over traffic flow and access policies.

GRE also enhances the flexibility of network design in hybrid environments by enabling overlay networking. Overlays built with GRE can span across cloud regions, connect to private data centers, and reach mobile or temporary sites with minimal configuration changes. This is particularly advantageous when deploying disaster recovery solutions, testing environments, or temporary connectivity for mergers and acquisitions. The agility provided by GRE overlays allows businesses to respond quickly to changing requirements without waiting for physical network changes or service provider intervention. These virtual links are entirely software-defined, making them easy to automate, replicate, and manage through orchestration tools and network controllers.

In terms of performance, GRE tunnels introduce some overhead due to encapsulation, which must be considered when designing hybrid environments. The added headers reduce the effective MTU, potentially leading to fragmentation if not properly addressed. Network administrators often implement Path MTU Discovery and adjust TCP MSS values to avoid issues related to large packet sizes. Additionally, monitoring tools can be employed to track tunnel health, latency, and throughput, ensuring that the performance impact of GRE encapsulation is minimized. Despite this overhead, the benefits of centralized management, secure transport, and flexible routing often outweigh the performance trade-offs, especially when the alternative is less predictable or less secure connectivity.

Scalability is another important factor in hybrid deployments, and GRE contributes positively in this area. Tunnels can be easily added or removed as new sites come online or as old sites are decommissioned. In large-scale deployments, GRE tunnels can be aggregated through hub-and-spoke topologies or mesh architectures, depending on the performance and redundancy needs. Hub-and-spoke designs, where all remote sites connect to a central core location, simplify configuration and policy enforcement. On the other hand, full mesh topologies enable direct site-to-site communication, reducing latency and avoiding bottlenecks. These design choices can be implemented incrementally, giving organizations the freedom to grow their hybrid network at their own pace.

Hybrid environments are also prone to changes in topology and policy due to the rapid evolution of business needs and technology. GRE tunnels provide a level of abstraction that shields network operations from the volatility of the underlying transport. Whether the connection traverses the public internet, a leased MPLS circuit, or a cloud interconnect, the GRE tunnel remains functionally consistent. This abstraction enables more predictable behavior and eases the implementation of consistent security, QoS, and routing policies across environments. Policy enforcement points can be placed at the GRE endpoints, where firewall rules, NAT, and traffic shaping can be applied before encapsulation or after decapsulation, ensuring that policies remain intact regardless of the transport path.

An increasingly common pattern in secure hybrid deployments is the use of GRE tunnels to connect to cloud-based firewalls or secure web gateways. These tunnels route enterprise-bound or internet-bound traffic through centralized inspection points, where security policies are enforced uniformly. This model ensures compliance with corporate governance, data loss prevention rules, and threat protection measures while leveraging the elasticity of the cloud. By using GRE to transport traffic to these inspection points, organizations retain control over how and where their traffic is analyzed without being limited by native cloud routing capabilities.

GRE has proven to be a versatile and essential technology for secure hybrid deployments, bridging disparate environments into a unified and secure network fabric. It empowers organizations to preserve the control and complexity of their on-premises networks while extending seamlessly into the cloud. Through its support for encapsulation, dynamic routing, and secure transport when paired with IPsec, GRE addresses the critical challenges of modern hybrid architectures. As the demand for agile, secure, and scalable connectivity continues to grow, GRE will remain a foundational element in building resilient hybrid networks that meet the performance, security, and flexibility needs of the modern enterprise.

GRE and SD-WAN Compatibility

As enterprise networking continues to evolve toward greater flexibility, agility, and cost-efficiency, Software-Defined Wide Area Networking, or SD-WAN, has emerged as a transformative solution. SD-WAN simplifies the management and operation of a WAN by decoupling the control and data planes, enabling centralized control, dynamic path selection, and application-aware routing. At the same time, many enterprises continue to rely on traditional technologies such as Generic Routing Encapsulation, or GRE, which provides a reliable and widely supported mechanism for creating point-to-point tunnels across IP networks. The question of compatibility between GRE and SD-WAN arises frequently, particularly in hybrid deployments where legacy infrastructure and modern SD-WAN solutions must coexist. Understanding how GRE and SD-WAN can interoperate is essential for designing scalable, secure, and high-performing network architectures that leverage the strengths of both technologies.

GRE provides a lightweight, protocol-independent tunneling method that encapsulates a wide variety of network layer protocols inside IP tunnels. This encapsulation enables the creation of virtual point-to-point links between endpoints, allowing organizations to extend private networks across public or shared infrastructure. In contrast, SD-WAN uses overlay tunnels that often rely on more advanced encapsulation formats such as VXLAN, IPsec, or proprietary protocols that support dynamic routing, load balancing, traffic prioritization, and performance monitoring. Despite these architectural differences, GRE can complement SD-WAN by serving as an additional transport mechanism or by connecting non-SD-WAN capable devices to the SD-WAN fabric.

One of the primary areas of compatibility between GRE and SD-WAN lies in their shared ability to abstract the underlying transport network. GRE tunnels can traverse the same broadband or MPLS circuits that an SD-WAN solution uses, allowing for the coexistence of traditional routing protocols and modern SD-WAN control mechanisms. For example, an enterprise may deploy SD-WAN for branch connectivity while maintaining GRE tunnels to connect legacy systems, third-party networks, or monitoring tools that require a stable, direct tunnel. In this way, GRE becomes a parallel overlay that serves specific use cases not directly supported by the SD-WAN platform, preserving the investment in existing infrastructure.

GRE can also be used to extend SD-WAN connectivity into environments that are not natively SD-WAN capable. Some legacy routers or network appliances may not support SD-WAN features but still need to participate in a broader network topology. By establishing GRE tunnels from these legacy devices to SD-WAN edge nodes or controllers, administrators can integrate them into the SD-WAN fabric without requiring hardware upgrades or software modifications. These GRE tunnels act as transport pipes that deliver traffic to SD-WAN entry points, where it can then be inspected, classified, and routed according to the SD-WAN policies. This model is particularly useful in mergers and acquisitions, where different network technologies must be unified quickly.

Another compatibility consideration is the ability of SD-WAN solutions to recognize and manage GRE-encapsulated traffic. Some SD-WAN platforms are capable of detecting GRE headers and treating the encapsulated packets as separate traffic classes. This enables administrators to apply quality of service (QoS), path selection, and prioritization policies based on the inner packet contents or the GRE source and destination. When properly configured, GRE tunnels running over SD-WAN can benefit from all the performance optimization features the SD-WAN offers, including dynamic path selection, packet duplication, forward error correction, and jitter mitigation. These capabilities are crucial for applications such as VoIP, video conferencing, or real-time collaboration tools that are sensitive to latency and packet loss.

There are also deployment models where GRE tunnels are used within the SD-WAN fabric itself. Some SD-WAN vendors use GRE as a transport protocol for their overlay tunnels, taking advantage of GRE's simplicity and low overhead. In these cases, GRE serves as a wrapper for encrypted or optimized traffic, providing the foundation upon which the SD-WAN builds its control and data plane functionalities. This is especially common in platforms that use GRE combined with IPsec, offering a secure and efficient encapsulation method that aligns with performance and security requirements. By using GRE internally, SD-WAN solutions can maintain vendor interoperability and simplify tunnel management.

Security is a key consideration in any discussion about compatibility. GRE by itself lacks encryption, authentication, and integrity checking, which are critical features in secure network environments. SD-WAN platforms, however, typically include strong security features such as integrated IPsec encryption, firewall services, and application-layer inspection. When GRE is used in conjunction with SD-WAN, it must be secured either through GRE over IPsec or by ensuring that the GRE tunnels operate entirely within the trusted boundaries of the SD-WAN overlay. This hybrid security model ensures that sensitive data remains protected without sacrificing the flexibility that GRE offers. In high-security environments, GRE may also be used to carry isolated or segregated traffic that is then encrypted and inspected by SD-WAN security mechanisms.

Operational visibility and monitoring are other areas where GRE and SD-WAN must be harmonized. SD-WAN platforms provide extensive telemetry, performance analytics, and centralized dashboards that allow administrators to monitor traffic flows and tunnel health in real-time. When GRE tunnels are integrated into the SD-WAN topology, it becomes necessary to ensure that GRE-specific metrics are also captured and reported. This can be achieved by configuring the SD-WAN platform to recognize GRE flows, track their performance, and correlate them with overall application behavior. This unified visibility helps in troubleshooting, capacity planning, and performance tuning, ensuring that GRE traffic is not treated as opaque or unmanaged.

From a design perspective, network architects must carefully consider how GRE tunnels are integrated with SD-WAN to avoid redundancy or routing conflicts. GRE tunnels introduce an additional layer of routing and encapsulation, which, if not properly aligned with SD-WAN policies, can lead to asymmetric routing, MTU issues, or policy misalignment. Best practices include defining clear traffic segmentation rules, aligning routing advertisements, and ensuring consistent MTU handling across GRE and SD-WAN interfaces. In some cases, route redistribution may be used to advertise GRE-reachable subnets into the SD-WAN fabric or vice versa, enabling seamless interoperation between the two domains.

In hybrid enterprise networks where change is constant and requirements vary widely, the compatibility between GRE and SD-WAN offers a bridge between traditional and modern networking paradigms. GRE provides the raw tunneling capability needed to support legacy applications, flexible routing, and broad protocol support, while SD-WAN delivers centralized control, intelligent traffic management, and robust security. Their combined use enables enterprises to evolve their networks incrementally, ensuring business continuity while embracing the advantages of digital transformation. As networking technologies continue to converge and diversify, the strategic integration of GRE within SD-WAN architectures will remain a valuable option for achieving scalable, secure, and adaptable connectivity.

GRE Loop Prevention Techniques

In complex networking environments, the use of Generic Routing Encapsulation, or GRE, can introduce unexpected behaviors if not designed with care, particularly when it comes to the prevention of routing loops. GRE tunnels create virtual point-to-point links that encapsulate packets for transport across an IP network. While this mechanism is highly flexible and supports a wide range of use cases, it also introduces an additional layer of abstraction in the routing topology, which can lead to scenarios where traffic continuously circulates between GRE endpoints due to incorrect or ambiguous routing information. These routing loops can consume bandwidth, increase CPU load on routers, and ultimately lead to network instability or even outages. As such, understanding and implementing GRE loop prevention techniques is essential for maintaining the health and reliability of the network.

One of the primary contributors to GRE loops is the recursive routing problem. Recursive routing occurs when the route to the GRE tunnel destination is learned through the tunnel itself. In this situation, a router might attempt to send encapsulated packets into a GRE tunnel whose endpoint is reachable only through that same tunnel, creating a loop condition. This recursive dependency can trigger repeated encapsulation and forwarding of packets, consuming router resources and potentially leading to a routing black hole. To avoid this, network administrators must ensure that the GRE tunnel destination is reachable via a physical interface or through a separate logical path that does not depend on the tunnel. This design principle ensures that packets destined for the tunnel endpoint never enter the tunnel during path resolution.

Another effective technique to prevent GRE loops involves the use of routing protocol filtering and policy control. In networks where dynamic routing protocols such as OSPF or BGP are used over GRE tunnels, route filtering plays a critical role in ensuring that routes learned through a GRE tunnel are not redistributed in a way that causes them to be advertised back into the same tunnel. For instance, if a router learns a prefix through a GRE tunnel and then advertises that prefix back to the remote endpoint via the same tunnel, it creates the potential for a loop. Administrators must implement prefix-lists, route-maps, or policy statements that explicitly control which routes are advertised or accepted through the tunnel. This granular control over routing information exchange is fundamental in breaking potential loop paths and maintaining deterministic route propagation.

Loop prevention also relies on the careful use of tunnel-specific metrics and routing preferences. GRE tunnel interfaces should be assigned metrics or administrative distances that reflect their intended role within the routing topology. By ensuring that GRE routes are preferred only when appropriate and not as a default path, administrators can prevent inadvertent selection of a GRE tunnel as the best route for traffic that should traverse a different interface. Manipulating route preferences using metrics or weight values allows for a controlled routing hierarchy, where GRE tunnels are used only for specific destinations or under defined conditions. This technique not only avoids loops but also helps optimize traffic flow and redundancy.

GRE loop prevention is further enhanced by monitoring and controlling the encapsulation depth. Some routers implement a limit on the number of times a packet can be encapsulated in a GRE tunnel. This encapsulation limit is a safety feature that prevents packets from being repeatedly re-encapsulated in a loop, ultimately being discarded when the limit is reached. While not a substitute for proper design, this mechanism acts as a last-resort safeguard to prevent infinite loops from overwhelming the network. Administrators can configure encapsulation thresholds or leverage Time-To-Live (TTL) values in GRE packets to detect and suppress looping traffic. By decrementing TTL at each hop and discarding packets when TTL reaches zero, the network ensures that no packet can circulate indefinitely.

Network segmentation and topology planning also play a pivotal role in GRE loop prevention. Designing clear boundaries between routing domains and tunnel termination points reduces the chance of circular routing paths. GRE tunnels should be part of a hierarchical or layered network design, where their role and reachability are well-defined. This includes using unique addressing schemes for GRE tunnel endpoints and avoiding address overlap or ambiguity. Separating control-plane traffic used for tunnel maintenance from the data-plane traffic transported inside the tunnel can also reduce complexity and mitigate the risk of loops. When the control path is isolated, it becomes easier to trace and validate routing decisions that affect GRE traffic.

Monitoring tools and diagnostic techniques are indispensable for detecting and addressing GRE loops. Packet capture tools, traceroute, and GRE-specific debugging commands help visualize the flow of encapsulated traffic and identify anomalies. Sudden increases in tunnel traffic, unexplained latency, or CPU spikes on routing devices may indicate a loop condition. By analyzing packet headers and routing tables, administrators can pinpoint the origin of the loop and apply corrective actions. Real-time telemetry, NetFlow data, and SNMP alerts provide early warnings and insights into tunnel health, enabling proactive loop detection before it impacts end users.

GRE loop prevention is not a single configuration or setting but a multifaceted strategy that combines thoughtful design, strict routing control, and continuous monitoring. Each GRE deployment must be carefully analyzed within the context of the broader network topology to ensure that traffic flows are predictable and loops are structurally impossible. By separating routing paths, using appropriate metrics, applying route filters, and leveraging platform-specific safeguards, network engineers can build robust GRE tunnel implementations that deliver the intended functionality without risking instability. As GRE continues to serve as a foundational tunneling technology in hybrid, cloud, and multi-domain environments, its secure and stable operation depends on meticulous planning and disciplined management of loop prevention techniques.

Redundancy and Failover in GRE

Generic Routing Encapsulation, or GRE, is widely used in enterprise and service provider networks to create virtual point-to-point tunnels that transport encapsulated packets over IP networks. Its flexibility allows the transport of multicast, non-IP traffic, and various routing protocols, making it a go-to solution for many network architects. However, GRE by itself lacks inherent mechanisms for redundancy and failover, which are critical components in high-availability network designs. Ensuring that GRE tunnels remain reliable in the face of link or device failure requires careful design, strategic use of routing protocols, and the implementation of failover techniques that minimize disruption and ensure continuity of service.

In a typical GRE deployment, a tunnel is established between two endpoints, creating a logical path through which traffic flows. While this setup works well under normal conditions, it introduces a single point of failure. If either of the tunnel endpoints becomes unreachable or if the path between them is interrupted, the GRE tunnel collapses, and any data relying on it for transport is lost. To mitigate this risk, redundancy must be introduced at various levels: physical interface, logical path, routing protocol, and tunnel configuration.

The most fundamental approach to redundancy in GRE involves the creation of multiple tunnels between different endpoints or over diverse paths. This can be accomplished by configuring secondary GRE tunnels with distinct source and destination IP addresses that follow alternate routes through the network. These tunnels can be kept as hot standbys or load-balanced through routing metrics. By advertising the same destination prefixes over different tunnels with varying route preferences or administrative distances, failover can be orchestrated seamlessly. In the event that the primary GRE tunnel becomes unavailable, dynamic routing protocols like OSPF or BGP can detect the failure and reroute traffic through the backup tunnel. This automatic rerouting depends heavily on timely detection of tunnel health and rapid convergence of the routing protocol in use.

GRE tunnel interfaces themselves do not participate in link-layer keepalive mechanisms like physical interfaces do, so their operational status may not accurately reflect connectivity to the remote endpoint. To address this, GRE keepalives can be configured. This feature allows GRE routers to send periodic keepalive packets through the tunnel to the far end and wait for a response. If the expected response is not received within a configured interval, the tunnel interface is marked down. This status change can trigger routing protocol convergence and shift traffic to an alternate path. GRE keepalives thus simulate link status and provide a mechanism for faster detection of failure, enabling more responsive failover.

An alternative or complementary technique to GRE keepalives is the use of Bidirectional Forwarding Detection, or BFD. BFD is a lightweight protocol designed to detect faults between two forwarding engines connected by a link. When implemented alongside GRE, BFD offers faster failure detection than GRE keepalives, typically in the sub-second range. BFD sessions are established over the GRE tunnel and monitored continuously. If the BFD session fails, the associated routing protocol is immediately notified, and failover can be initiated. BFD provides the necessary precision and speed for networks that require minimal downtime and rapid response to outages.

Failover behavior is also influenced by the choice of routing protocol and how routes are advertised. In multi-tunnel scenarios, administrators can manipulate route preferences using metrics, weights, or local preference values. For example, in an OSPF environment, the cost associated with each GRE tunnel interface can be adjusted so that one path is preferred under normal circumstances, and others are used only when the preferred path becomes unavailable. In a BGP setup, route attributes like MED or AS path can be used to influence outbound or inbound route selection. This level of control allows for deterministic failover, ensuring that traffic is rerouted according to policy rather than simply defaulting to any available path.

Redundancy can also be achieved through equal-cost multipath routing, or ECMP. If multiple GRE tunnels are available with identical routing metrics, the routing protocol may treat them as equal-cost paths and distribute traffic among them. This not only provides redundancy but also enables load balancing, increasing throughput and resource utilization. If one of the tunnels fails, traffic is redistributed across the remaining operational paths without requiring full routing convergence. ECMP thus offers both resilience and performance benefits, provided the underlying platform supports per-packet or per-flow load balancing over GRE tunnels.

Another aspect of failover involves physical and interface-level redundancy. GRE tunnels rely on the underlying physical or virtual interfaces for packet transport. If an interface goes down, the tunnel depending on it becomes unreachable. To mitigate this, redundant physical interfaces can be grouped into port-channels or bonded links. These aggregated links provide link-level redundancy, where the failure of one member does not affect overall connectivity. GRE tunnels sourced from such resilient interfaces benefit indirectly from hardware-level fault tolerance, reducing the likelihood of tunnel disruption due to hardware failure.

In some deployments, tunnel redundancy is implemented using dynamic tunnel creation or orchestration tools that instantiate GRE tunnels on demand. This approach is often used in cloud or virtualized environments, where endpoints and network paths are ephemeral. Network controllers or automation frameworks monitor connectivity and spin up GRE tunnels only when required, ensuring efficient use of resources and high availability. These dynamically created tunnels are typically integrated with SDN controllers that have global visibility of the network state, allowing them to make intelligent decisions about failover and traffic redirection.

Monitoring and alerting systems play an important role in GRE redundancy and failover strategy. Network administrators must have visibility into tunnel health, performance metrics, and routing behavior to proactively address issues before they affect users. Tools such as SNMP, NetFlow, telemetry, and custom scripts can be used to monitor tunnel status and generate alerts. When a tunnel goes down or becomes degraded, automated systems can trigger configuration changes, reroute traffic, or escalate issues to network operations teams.

Designing redundancy and failover mechanisms for GRE is not merely about creating backup tunnels; it involves a holistic approach that includes failure detection, routing protocol behavior, interface management, and monitoring. A successful GRE deployment incorporates multiple layers of protection and ensures that network traffic continues to flow smoothly, even when parts of the infrastructure experience failure. Whether supporting branch-to-data center communication, inter-cloud connectivity, or secure remote access, GRE tunnels must be engineered with failover in mind to deliver the high availability expected in modern networks. Through proper planning and the use of complementary technologies, GRE can be made as resilient and dependable as any physical connection, forming the backbone of robust and redundant network architectures.

Load Balancing Across GRE Tunnels

Generic Routing Encapsulation, or GRE, provides a flexible method for creating virtual point-to-point links over IP networks. While GRE is often implemented for extending private networks, supporting routing protocols, or transporting multicast and non-IP traffic, it is also an effective mechanism when multiple tunnels are required to support scalability, fault tolerance, and efficient bandwidth utilization. Load balancing across GRE tunnels introduces a method for distributing traffic across multiple GRE links in order to optimize performance, reduce congestion, and ensure redundancy. However, this requires careful planning and a deep understanding of how routers make forwarding decisions in the presence of multiple available paths.

At its core, GRE is a simple encapsulation protocol that wraps original packets inside a GRE header and an outer IP header. When multiple GRE tunnels are established between two or more locations, they essentially create several parallel paths that can be used to transport data. These tunnels may traverse different physical circuits, ISPs, or even geographic routes. Without a load balancing mechanism in place, traffic might default to using a single tunnel, leaving other tunnels underutilized or reserved only for failover. By leveraging dynamic routing protocols and the underlying platform's ability to support equal-cost multipath routing, or ECMP, it becomes possible to distribute traffic across these GRE tunnels in an efficient and predictable way.

ECMP is a common method for achieving load balancing when multiple paths to the same destination exist with equal cost. Routing protocols such as OSPF and EIGRP can be configured to view GRE tunnels as interfaces with identical metrics, allowing them to install multiple next hops for the same destination prefix into the routing table. The forwarding engine then balances traffic across the available tunnels based on a predefined algorithm. Depending on the platform and configuration, this algorithm might operate on a per-packet, per-flow, or per-destination basis. Each method has implications for performance and consistency. Per-packet load balancing distributes packets in a round-robin fashion, which can lead to packet reordering in applications sensitive to sequence. Per-flow load balancing, often based on a hash of source and destination IP addresses and ports, preserves the order of packets within each session, making it more suitable for real-time applications such as VoIP or video.

To implement load balancing across GRE tunnels, the first step is ensuring that each tunnel is operational and has a unique source and destination pair. Routers must be configured so that routing protocols see each GRE tunnel as a viable path with equal cost. This might require setting consistent tunnel interface metrics, adjusting OSPF cost values, or manipulating EIGRP delay parameters. Once this is in place, routers will install multiple equal-cost routes in the forwarding table, and the forwarding engine will begin distributing traffic across all active tunnels. This strategy increases aggregate throughput and provides resilience, as the failure of one tunnel will only reduce capacity rather than sever connectivity entirely.

An important aspect of successful GRE load balancing is the underlying platform's support for hardware-assisted forwarding. Software-based routers may struggle to efficiently balance traffic across multiple tunnels due to CPU limitations, especially when per-packet balancing is used. Routers equipped with specialized forwarding ASICs or NPUs are better suited for handling large volumes of encapsulated traffic without introducing latency or jitter. This consideration becomes critical in data centers or service provider environments where GRE tunnels are used to transport high-bandwidth traffic between core locations.

Another dimension to GRE load balancing is path diversity. For true load balancing benefits, GRE tunnels must traverse different physical or logical paths. If multiple tunnels share the same underlying route through the internet or a carrier network, then the benefits of load balancing are diminished, and all tunnels are equally affected by congestion or failure. Path diversity ensures that traffic has alternative options during disruption and allows for better utilization of available bandwidth across links. Network architects should work with service providers to ensure that GRE tunnel endpoints are provisioned over distinct circuits or access methods.

In certain cases, administrators may wish to implement policy-based routing in conjunction with GRE tunnels to achieve more granular traffic distribution. Policy-based routing allows specific types of traffic to be directed through specific GRE tunnels based on criteria such as source or destination IP address, protocol, or application port. This technique can be used to separate critical applications from bulk traffic, route latency-sensitive traffic over lower-delay paths, or comply with regulatory and security constraints. When combined with load balancing principles, policy-based routing adds a layer of control that ensures traffic distribution aligns with business objectives and performance expectations.

Monitoring and performance management are crucial for maintaining effective GRE load balancing. Tools such as NetFlow, IP SLA, SNMP, and telemetry provide visibility into tunnel utilization, latency, jitter, and packet loss. By continuously analyzing traffic patterns and tunnel behavior, administrators can detect imbalances, bottlenecks, or suboptimal routing decisions. Automated scripts and orchestration tools can be used to adjust tunnel metrics, bring up new tunnels, or tear down underutilized ones. This dynamic approach to GRE tunnel management ensures that load balancing remains effective as traffic demands change or as the network topology evolves.

Security considerations must also be taken into account when implementing GRE load balancing. Since GRE does not provide encryption, each tunnel must be evaluated for potential exposure to interception or spoofing. When GRE is used across untrusted networks such as the public internet, IPsec should be implemented to encrypt and authenticate GRE traffic. In a load-balanced configuration, each GRE tunnel must have a corresponding IPsec tunnel or be encapsulated within a shared IPsec transport. Coordinating IPsec policies across multiple tunnels adds complexity, especially when integrating dynamic key exchange protocols like IKEv2. Nevertheless, this step is essential for maintaining the confidentiality and integrity of data in a distributed GRE architecture.

In hybrid cloud environments, GRE load balancing facilitates seamless connectivity between on-premises data centers and multiple cloud regions or providers. By establishing multiple GRE tunnels to different cloud edge points, enterprises can distribute workloads, improve performance, and ensure failover capabilities. Load balancing across GRE tunnels in this context enhances user experience by reducing latency and increasing application availability. As more organizations adopt multi-cloud strategies, the ability to implement robust, scalable GRE-based transport between environments becomes increasingly important.

Ultimately, load balancing across GRE tunnels provides a scalable and resilient solution for modern networks that require high availability, performance, and flexibility. Through intelligent routing, thoughtful design, and continuous monitoring, administrators can leverage GRE's encapsulation capabilities while ensuring that traffic is efficiently distributed across multiple paths. This not only optimizes resource utilization but also strengthens the overall stability and responsiveness of the network infrastructure. As networks become more dynamic and distributed, the techniques and technologies behind GRE load balancing will remain an essential component of enterprise and service provider architectures.

GRE with VRF-Aware Routing

Generic Routing Encapsulation, or GRE, plays a vital role in enabling flexible network designs, particularly when combined with Virtual Routing and Forwarding, known as VRF. GRE provides a mechanism to encapsulate traffic between two points over an IP network, essentially creating a tunnel that behaves like a direct link. VRF, on the other hand, allows multiple instances of routing tables to coexist on the same physical router, enabling segmentation of traffic, isolation of routing domains, and support for multi-tenant or service-specific topologies. When these two technologies are used together, they offer a powerful solution for scalable, segmented, and secure IP transport. GRE with VRF-aware routing enables enterprises and service providers to extend isolated routing domains across Layer 3 networks while maintaining clear separation of control and data planes for each virtual network.

In traditional network architectures, GRE tunnels are often configured globally, meaning they operate within the default routing table. This setup is sufficient in simple environments where all routing information belongs to a single context. However, in complex deployments where multiple customers, business units, or services require routing separation, global tunnels become limiting. VRF-aware GRE tunnels address this limitation by binding each tunnel interface to a specific VRF instance. This allows the tunnel's routing, forwarding, and encapsulation behaviors to be governed entirely by the associated VRF, ensuring that traffic from different VRFs does not leak into one another's routing domains.

A practical example of GRE with VRF-aware routing occurs in multi-tenant environments. A service provider may host several customers, each requiring private Layer 3 connectivity to their remote sites. By assigning each customer to a separate VRF and configuring GRE tunnels within those VRFs, the provider can maintain complete routing isolation between tenants. Each VRF maintains its own routing table, and GRE tunnels serve as the transport for customer traffic between geographically dispersed locations. The source and destination of each GRE tunnel are VRF-specific, and routing updates exchanged over the tunnels pertain only to the associated VRF, thereby preserving the integrity and confidentiality of each customer's routing information.

From a technical standpoint, creating a GRE tunnel in a VRF context requires assigning the tunnel interface to a VRF and ensuring that its source and destination addresses are also reachable within that VRF. The tunnel's source IP address must belong to an interface assigned to the same VRF, and the remote endpoint must be resolvable through the VRF's routing table. This constraint ensures that the tunnel operates entirely within the VRF's scope, avoiding ambiguity in route resolution. Any dynamic routing protocol running over the GRE tunnel, such as OSPF or BGP, also functions in the context of the VRF, enabling seamless distribution of prefixes within the same virtual routing domain.

One significant advantage of GRE with VRF-aware routing is the ability to build hub-and-spoke or full-mesh topologies across VRF instances without relying on MPLS. This becomes especially useful in enterprises that do not have access to MPLS services but still require secure and isolated routing domains across multiple sites. Each site can have one or more GRE tunnels bound to VRF interfaces, enabling the construction of complex topologies while keeping customer or departmental traffic strictly segmented. In the absence of MPLS, GRE with VRF-aware routing becomes a cost-effective and flexible alternative to more expensive or restrictive transport technologies.

Another benefit is enhanced security through logical isolation. Because each VRF operates independently, even if two GRE tunnels share the same physical path or IP network, the traffic inside each tunnel remains logically isolated. Unauthorized access between VRFs is prevented by design, as the routing processes and forwarding decisions are bound to separate contexts. This is particularly important for organizations with strict regulatory or compliance requirements that mandate traffic separation, such as in healthcare, finance, or government networks.

Scalability is another key consideration. A large organization may need to support hundreds or even thousands of VRF-aware GRE tunnels. Most modern routers support per-VRF tunnel instantiation, where each VRF can maintain its own set of GRE tunnels, routing processes, and policies without impacting the global routing table. With appropriate hardware and software, GRE with VRF-aware routing can scale horizontally, enabling support for expansive multi-tenant or service-segmented designs. Each VRF can also have tailored policies, such as specific QoS configurations, routing filters, or security rules, allowing for highly customized treatment of traffic per logical instance.

The operational complexity of managing VRF-aware GRE tunnels requires robust automation and monitoring tools. Manually configuring each GRE tunnel in a VRF is error-prone and inefficient, especially in dynamic environments. Network automation platforms can simplify this process by using templates, APIs, and orchestration frameworks to deploy VRF-aware GRE configurations at scale. These tools can ensure consistency, validate tunnel health, and automatically push updates when endpoints or policies change. Additionally, telemetry and monitoring systems must be VRF-aware, capable of collecting and analyzing tunnel statistics, routing updates, and performance metrics on a per-VRF basis.

Troubleshooting VRF-aware GRE tunnels demands familiarity with both VRF and GRE internals. Because each tunnel exists in its own routing context, traditional global ping or traceroute commands may not yield accurate results. Network engineers must issue diagnostic commands within the appropriate VRF to verify tunnel reachability, resolve next-hop issues, or trace routing inconsistencies. Logically separating management tools and routing diagnostics by VRF ensures that each routing domain can be examined independently, reducing the risk of misdiagnosis or unintended changes that could affect other tenants or services.

As virtualized environments, cloud services, and containerized applications continue to grow, the demand for network segmentation and flexible overlay transport mechanisms also increases. GRE with VRF-aware routing provides a highly adaptable framework for interconnecting isolated routing domains across any IP network. It allows organizations to build scalable, secure, and customizable Layer 3 overlays that support the dynamic requirements of modern applications, multi-site deployments, and diverse customer use cases. The combination of GRE's tunneling capabilities with VRF's segmentation power enables a new level of architectural flexibility that aligns well with the direction of enterprise and service provider networking. As a result, GRE with VRF-aware routing will continue to play a critical role in next-generation network designs that demand both control and isolation across an ever-growing set of endpoints and services.

GRE in Virtualized Infrastructure

Generic Routing Encapsulation, or GRE, has long been a staple of network design due to its simplicity and flexibility in creating point-to-point tunnels across IP networks. As enterprise environments increasingly shift toward virtualization, GRE has proven to be just as valuable in virtualized infrastructures as it is in physical networks. In data centers and cloud environments where virtual machines, containers, and software-defined networking are now the norm, GRE enables seamless connectivity between distributed workloads, supports routing protocol exchanges, and facilitates the creation of isolated overlay networks. Its adaptability allows it to function as a foundational technology within virtualized systems, providing transport mechanisms that are independent of underlying physical topologies and highly compatible with modern orchestration tools.

In a virtualized infrastructure, physical network boundaries are abstracted, replaced by logical constructs such as virtual switches, virtual routers, and overlay networks. These abstractions allow for the creation of flexible, scalable, and rapidly deployable environments, but they also introduce new complexities in terms of routing, segmentation, and interconnectivity. GRE fills this gap by offering a lightweight tunneling method that can bridge isolated virtual networks, enabling communication between virtual machines running on different hosts, within different data centers, or even across cloud regions. This is particularly useful in scenarios where workloads must be migrated without changing their IP addressing schemes, or when legacy applications need to communicate securely and consistently across a virtual fabric.

One of the most common applications of GRE in virtualized infrastructures is in the implementation of overlays. Overlay networks are logical constructs that sit atop the physical underlay network and allow for segmentation, multi-tenancy, and flexible address management. GRE tunnels form the backbone of many such overlays, encapsulating traffic from tenant virtual machines and transporting it across the underlay network to remote endpoints. These tunnels allow network architects to build flat Layer 2 or routed Layer 3 topologies that span across disparate physical infrastructure without relying on complex VLAN stitching or proprietary solutions. Each GRE tunnel acts as a logical link between endpoints, enabling traffic to traverse multiple hypervisors, network fabrics, or cloud providers without modification to application configurations.

In addition to their role in overlays, GRE tunnels are instrumental in extending dynamic routing into virtualized environments. Virtual routers deployed as software appliances can use GRE to establish routing adjacencies with other routers across the data center or the cloud. These tunnels allow protocols like OSPF, BGP, or EIGRP to exchange route information across isolated domains, supporting automatic route propagation, failover, and policy-based forwarding. This becomes especially powerful in multi-tenant environments where each tenant might have its own virtual router instance with separate routing policies and tables. GRE tunnels help link these virtual routers into a cohesive architecture while maintaining routing independence.

Security within virtualized infrastructures is always a critical concern, and GRE supports several strategies to maintain data confidentiality and integrity. While GRE does not provide encryption natively, it is frequently paired with IPsec to create secure GRE-over-IPsec tunnels. This combination allows encrypted transport of GRE-encapsulated packets, making it possible to carry sensitive traffic across untrusted or shared infrastructure. In a cloud or multi-tenant environment, this ensures that tenant traffic remains isolated and secure, even if the GRE tunnels are riding over a common underlay network. Security policies can also be enforced at the tunnel endpoints, where virtual firewalls inspect and control encapsulated traffic before it enters or leaves a tunnel.

In containerized and microservices-based environments, GRE is used to facilitate service connectivity across clusters or across namespaces within a Kubernetes ecosystem. While container networks often use VXLAN or IP-in-IP for tunneling, GRE remains a viable alternative in environments where these methods are not supported or where GRE offers simpler integration with existing routing protocols. GRE tunnels can be established between container network interfaces, providing isolated communication channels between pods, services, or namespaces. This approach can support scenarios where specific microservices need to communicate across geographic boundaries or between on-premises data centers and cloud environments, ensuring consistent IP routing and policy enforcement across the network.

Another important benefit of GRE in virtualized environments is its compatibility with automation and orchestration platforms. GRE tunnels can be defined and deployed programmatically through scripts, APIs, or configuration management tools such as Ansible, Terraform, or vendor-specific controllers. This allows for rapid provisioning of network infrastructure in response to changes in workload placement or service demand. A newly instantiated virtual machine or containerized application can trigger the automatic creation of a GRE tunnel to connect it to its peers, enabling on-demand network expansion without manual intervention. This dynamic behavior aligns well with the elastic nature of cloud-native architectures, where resources are frequently scaled up or down based on real-time requirements.

Performance is another key consideration in virtualized environments, where network throughput and latency can impact application responsiveness and user experience. GRE encapsulation introduces some overhead, which must be accounted for in terms of MTU and CPU utilization. In virtual routers or software-based appliances, GRE processing relies on the host's resources, potentially introducing bottlenecks if not properly optimized. To mitigate this, administrators can tune GRE parameters such as TCP MSS and use hardware offloading features when supported by the hypervisor or the network interface card. Performance monitoring tools should also be GRE-aware, providing visibility into tunnel health, packet loss, latency, and jitter across the virtualized network.

Hybrid deployments involving both virtualized and physical infrastructure benefit significantly from GRE's bridging capabilities. GRE tunnels can connect virtual environments to physical routers, switches, or firewalls, enabling a unified network fabric that spans both realms. This is useful for scenarios such as branch office connectivity, where a physical router might establish GRE tunnels to a virtual appliance in the data center or the cloud. It also supports gradual migration strategies, where workloads are moved from physical to virtual environments without breaking existing network paths or access control policies. By abstracting the underlying transport, GRE provides a consistent mechanism for traffic forwarding that simplifies integration and transition.

GRE's role in virtualized infrastructure is foundational to enabling network designs that are flexible, scalable, and responsive to the dynamic nature of modern IT environments. It offers a universal tunneling solution that integrates smoothly with existing technologies, supports advanced routing and segmentation, and enables secure and programmable connectivity across diverse platforms. Whether used for extending routing domains, building overlays, securing tenant traffic, or supporting containerized applications, GRE continues to be a valuable tool in the arsenal of network architects working within the complex landscape of virtualization and cloud computing. As virtualized infrastructure continues to evolve, GRE's adaptability ensures it will remain relevant in supporting both legacy integration and forward-looking designs that demand agility and control.

GRE and Firewall Considerations

Generic Routing Encapsulation, or GRE, is a widely used tunneling protocol that enables the encapsulation of various network layer protocols within IP tunnels. It plays a crucial role in enterprise networks, allowing for the transport of multicast traffic, legacy protocols, and routing information between locations over an IP backbone. Despite its simplicity and flexibility, GRE poses unique challenges when it comes to integration with firewalls, particularly in environments where security policies must tightly control and inspect traffic. Firewalls, by their nature, are designed to evaluate and filter traffic based on known protocols and ports, applying deep inspection and enforcing policy across layers of the OSI model. GRE, however, operates differently from traditional TCP and UDP-based protocols, leading to specific considerations that network architects and security administrators must account for when deploying GRE in secure environments.

At the protocol level, GRE is classified as an IP protocol, specifically protocol number 47, rather than a protocol that relies on transport-layer ports like TCP or UDP. This means that firewalls must be explicitly configured to recognize and allow IP protocol 47 traffic in order for GRE tunnels to function correctly. Unlike TCP port 80 or UDP port 53, GRE's lack of port information makes it more challenging for firewalls to distinguish between different GRE sessions, especially in high-density environments with multiple tunnels. Firewalls that do not have native GRE awareness may block GRE packets by default, interpreting them as unfamiliar or potentially unsafe traffic. This often results in failed tunnel establishment or intermittent tunnel instability that can be difficult to diagnose without specific logging and packet inspection capabilities.

When GRE is used in conjunction with IPsec, as in GRE over IPsec configurations, the interaction with firewalls becomes more nuanced. IPsec typically uses UDP port 500 for Internet Key Exchange (IKE) and IP protocol 50 for Encapsulating Security Payload (ESP), depending on whether tunnel or transport mode is employed. In GRE over IPsec scenarios, the GRE traffic is encapsulated within the encrypted IPsec payload, rendering it invisible to intermediate firewalls. This effectively eliminates the need for the firewall to explicitly support GRE, provided that IPsec traffic is permitted and properly negotiated through security associations. However, this adds complexity to firewall rule sets, especially in scenarios where dynamic key exchange and tunnel negotiation must pass through stateful firewalls that perform packet inspection and NAT.

Network Address Translation, or NAT, presents another challenge for GRE traffic. Since GRE lacks transport-layer headers, it does not carry port information that traditional NAT devices rely on to track sessions and perform translation. Many basic NAT implementations are incapable of properly handling GRE, resulting in dropped packets or improperly translated addresses. Firewalls that support GRE-aware NAT must be used when tunneling through NAT environments, especially in branch office deployments where a GRE tunnel must traverse a firewall performing PAT or dynamic NAT. Some enterprise firewalls offer GRE fix-up or application layer gateway functions to manage these sessions, though support varies by vendor and device model.

From a security perspective, GRE poses inspection and control limitations because of its encapsulation nature. Many firewalls are designed to inspect the payload of IP packets at layers 4 through 7 to enforce security policies such as intrusion detection, malware scanning, application control, and data loss prevention. GRE tunnels, by encapsulating the entire IP packet including its headers, obscure this information from devices that do not perform GRE decapsulation. This can allow potentially malicious or unauthorized traffic to pass undetected through the firewall if it is encapsulated inside GRE. To address this, some advanced firewalls can perform GRE decapsulation as part of their inspection pipeline, exposing the inner packet for analysis and policy enforcement. However, this capability is not universal and may require additional licenses or processing resources.

Firewall placement in the network topology is also a critical consideration. If a firewall is placed between GRE tunnel endpoints, it must be configured to allow GRE traffic bidirectionally and to manage session state appropriately. Stateful firewalls that track connections must be able to identify GRE flows and associate return traffic correctly. Stateless packet filters are simpler but offer less protection and do not maintain session information, which can impact GRE performance and reliability. In complex network topologies, firewalls may sit at the edge of multiple routing domains, requiring careful coordination between GRE tunnel routing and firewall policies to prevent asymmetric routing and unintended drops.

Another consideration is the impact of firewall logging and monitoring on GRE traffic visibility. Because GRE encapsulates entire IP packets, firewall logs that do not support GRE awareness may show limited or misleading information about the actual traffic being transported. This complicates troubleshooting, auditing, and compliance reporting. Security administrators may need to deploy out-of-band packet capture tools or configure GRE-aware flow exporters to obtain meaningful visibility into the types of applications, users, and destinations involved in the tunneled traffic. Where possible, logging policies should be updated to include GRE tunnel initiation, termination, and errors, enabling more complete forensic and operational insights.

Performance can also be affected when GRE traffic passes through firewalls that are not optimized for handling encapsulated protocols. Some firewall devices process GRE traffic in software rather than hardware, resulting in higher CPU utilization and potential bottlenecks. This can degrade tunnel throughput and increase latency, particularly when multiple GRE sessions are active or when large payloads are encapsulated. Network engineers must consider the hardware capabilities of their firewalls when designing GRE-heavy topologies and ensure that throughput, tunnel count, and concurrent session capacity are within supported thresholds. Load testing and validation in a lab environment before production deployment can help identify potential performance bottlenecks early in the design process.

Policy enforcement must be carefully defined in GRE environments to ensure that only authorized tunnels are permitted and that misuse of GRE for bypassing security controls is prevented. This includes applying access control lists or firewall rules that restrict GRE traffic to known source and destination IP addresses, as well as limiting the networks that can be encapsulated within tunnels. In environments where GRE is not required, it is advisable to block GRE traffic explicitly to reduce the attack surface and eliminate the risk of rogue tunneling. Where GRE is permitted, firewall policies should be supplemented by tunnel authentication and encryption, either through GRE-over-IPsec or through endpoint security controls that validate tunnel peers before allowing traffic.

GRE's role as a transport mechanism within modern networks brings both opportunities and challenges when integrated with firewalls. The flexibility GRE offers in creating overlays, supporting routing protocols, and transporting non-IP traffic is balanced by the need for careful firewall configuration, inspection capabilities, and performance considerations. As networks become more segmented, distributed, and dynamic, the intersection of tunneling and security becomes increasingly critical. Firewalls must evolve to handle protocols like GRE not only at a basic pass/block level but also in terms of session management, deep packet inspection, and compliance visibility. Through deliberate planning and informed design, GRE and firewalls can coexist effectively, ensuring both connectivity and security in even the most complex environments.

GRE with NAT Traversal

Generic Routing Encapsulation, or GRE, is a versatile tunneling protocol that allows the encapsulation of various Layer 3 protocols within IP packets, enabling the creation of point-to-point links over IP networks. While GRE is widely used in enterprise and service provider environments to support routing protocol adjacency, transport multicast traffic, and extend network segments, it encounters significant challenges when deployed in environments that use Network Address Translation, or NAT. NAT, which modifies IP address information in packet headers to facilitate private-to-public address translation, is pervasive in modern networks, especially in branch offices, residential deployments, and cloud environments. However, the stateless nature of GRE and its lack of port information make it inherently incompatible with traditional NAT mechanisms. This has led to the need for specific strategies and adaptations to allow GRE tunnels to traverse NAT devices effectively.

The core issue with GRE and NAT arises from the fundamental differences in how each operates. NAT devices, especially those performing Port Address Translation (PAT), track sessions based on IP addresses and transport layer port numbers. For protocols like TCP and UDP, this is straightforward because each session includes source and destination ports, allowing the NAT device to create unique translation entries. GRE, in contrast, is an IP protocol with protocol number 47 and does not use port numbers. It encapsulates packets with an additional IP header and a GRE header but does not provide transport-layer information that a NAT device can use to distinguish between multiple GRE sessions. This absence of ports means that NAT devices cannot track GRE sessions in the same way they track TCP or UDP connections, making it difficult to translate and forward GRE traffic correctly.

In scenarios where GRE must operate through a NAT device, the first consideration is whether the NAT device supports GRE passthrough. Some enterprise-grade firewalls and routers offer built-in support for GRE, allowing the device to recognize GRE protocol 47 and maintain a state table for the GRE session. This capability, often referred to as GRE fix-up or GRE ALG (Application Layer Gateway), enables the NAT device to track and forward GRE packets properly by associating them with internal hosts. However, support for GRE passthrough is not universal and may vary by device model, firmware version, or vendor. In networks where the NAT device does not support GRE, packets may be silently dropped, or the tunnel may fail to establish or remain unstable during operation.

Another challenge in GRE and NAT traversal involves multiple internal devices attempting to establish GRE tunnels through a single NAT device. Since GRE lacks port numbers, the NAT device cannot differentiate between two GRE sessions originating from different internal IPs but destined for the same public endpoint. This results in ambiguity in the NAT translation table, potentially causing packets to be misrouted or delivered to the wrong internal host. In such cases, NAT traversal for GRE is inherently limited to one active session per public IP address unless advanced mechanisms like one-to-one NAT or GRE-aware session tracking are in place.

To overcome these challenges, one of the most common solutions is to encapsulate GRE within a protocol that is NAT-friendly. GRE over IPsec is a widely adopted method that wraps the GRE packet in an IPsec tunnel, which itself is encapsulated using UDP or ESP. When IPsec is configured in transport mode with GRE, the GRE traffic is encrypted and transmitted within IPsec packets, allowing it to pass through NAT devices that support IPsec NAT traversal, or NAT-T. IPsec NAT-T uses UDP port 4500, making it compatible with most NAT devices, which can track and translate the session based on the UDP headers. This encapsulation hides the GRE payload from the NAT device while maintaining session integrity and allowing successful traversal.

In cloud and hybrid environments where NAT is unavoidable, such as in public cloud instances behind cloud-native NAT gateways, using GRE over IPsec becomes not just a best practice but often a requirement. Cloud NAT devices typically do not support raw GRE traffic, making native GRE tunneling infeasible without additional encapsulation. Deploying virtual network appliances that support GRE over IPsec allows administrators to extend on-premises routing domains into the cloud without relying on cloud-native VPN constructs that might not support advanced routing protocols or multicast traffic. These virtual routers or firewalls act as GRE tunnel endpoints, with IPsec providing encryption and NAT traversal capabilities.

An alternative strategy involves using other tunneling mechanisms designed with NAT traversal in mind, such as IP-in-UDP or L2TP. Some network architectures replace GRE entirely in NAT-constrained environments in favor of these protocols, which provide similar encapsulation functionality but include NAT-friendly transport layer information. While this approach avoids the complexities of GRE and NAT interaction, it requires adjustments in routing configuration, application expectations, and potentially the removal of GRE-specific features that may be essential in certain deployments.

Network design also plays a role in simplifying GRE and NAT interaction. Where possible, assigning public IP addresses to GRE tunnel endpoints can eliminate the need for NAT traversal entirely. This is practical in data center environments or enterprise edge routers with available public IP space. Even in constrained environments, allocating one-to-one static NAT entries can allow GRE traffic to pass unimpeded by associating a specific internal IP with a unique public IP, avoiding the ambiguity caused by multiple GRE sessions behind a single address. While this approach consumes more public IP addresses, it can significantly reduce operational complexity and improve tunnel reliability.

From a security standpoint, encapsulating GRE for NAT traversal also brings additional benefits. When using GRE over IPsec, data is encrypted and authenticated, protecting it from eavesdropping and tampering while also satisfying compliance requirements in regulated industries. The use of NAT-T ensures compatibility with intermediate firewalls and network devices, while IPsec security associations control access to the GRE tunnel endpoints. Firewalls can be configured to allow only specific GRE-over-IPsec sessions, reducing the attack surface and preventing unauthorized tunneling activity.

Monitoring and troubleshooting GRE tunnels through NAT require specific tools and methods. Packet captures, firewall logs, and tunnel status indicators help diagnose connectivity issues, identify packet drops, or confirm successful NAT traversal. Logging tools should be configured to track GRE protocol 47 activity, if supported, and to correlate GRE session failures with NAT translation failures or misconfigurations. Automated scripts and network management platforms can test tunnel availability and report on NAT traversal status in real time, supporting proactive network operations and rapid incident resolution.

GRE with NAT traversal is a critical consideration in modern network architectures, where the intersection of tunneling and address translation is increasingly common. By understanding the protocol limitations, leveraging compatible encapsulation methods such as IPsec, and designing network paths that account for NAT behavior, administrators can successfully deploy GRE in environments that were previously considered incompatible. These strategies ensure that GRE continues to serve as a reliable and flexible transport mechanism, even in complex topologies that include private addressing, dynamic translations, and security policies designed for traditional IP traffic.

GRE and IPv6 Transition Mechanisms

The transition from IPv4 to IPv6 presents one of the most significant architectural shifts in the history of networking. As IPv4 address exhaustion continues to drive the adoption of IPv6, many enterprises and service providers find themselves operating dual-stack environments where both protocols coexist. During this transitional period, it is essential to establish mechanisms that allow IPv4 and IPv6 systems to interoperate effectively. Generic Routing Encapsulation, or GRE, serves as one of the most flexible and widely adopted tools for enabling seamless communication between IPv4 and IPv6 networks. GRE provides a method for encapsulating packets from one protocol inside packets of another, allowing IPv6 traffic to be carried over IPv4 infrastructure and vice versa. This ability to encapsulate and transport one protocol within another is fundamental to many transition strategies, especially when native dual-stack operation is not feasible.

GRE's versatility stems from its protocol-independent design. It can encapsulate any Layer 3 protocol, including both IPv4 and IPv6, making it a natural fit for bridging networks that use different IP versions. For example, a GRE tunnel can be created between two IPv6 islands separated by an IPv4-only network. In this case, the IPv6 packets are encapsulated within GRE and transported over the IPv4 backbone without requiring the intermediate devices to understand or process IPv6. This technique allows organizations to deploy IPv6 incrementally while leveraging their existing IPv4 infrastructure, reducing the need for immediate, large-scale upgrades and providing a stable environment for gradual IPv6 integration.

GRE also enables tunneling of IPv4 traffic over IPv6 networks, a scenario that becomes increasingly relevant as more backbone providers and cloud platforms deploy IPv6 as the default transport protocol. In such cases, GRE tunnels can be configured with IPv6 source and destination addresses, encapsulating IPv4 traffic and enabling legacy systems to communicate over a modern IPv6 underlay. This approach is particularly useful in hybrid deployments where IPv6 has been deployed in certain segments of the network but IPv4 remains prevalent in others. GRE's ability to reverse the encapsulation direction based on deployment needs makes it a cornerstone of flexible transition planning.

One of the primary advantages of using GRE in IPv6 transition mechanisms is the preservation of routing protocol compatibility. Many dynamic routing protocols, such as OSPF, EIGRP, and BGP, were initially designed for IPv4 and later extended to support IPv6. In cases where routing domains must exchange IPv6 prefixes but cannot support native adjacency over an IPv4 backbone, GRE tunnels enable the formation of routing adjacencies over an IPv4 transport. This allows for full exchange of IPv6 routes between islands, maintaining dynamic, fault-tolerant routing without requiring the entire backbone to operate in dual-stack mode. By creating virtual links using GRE tunnels, routing protocols can operate as though they are directly connected, even across infrastructure that does not natively support the desired protocol.

GRE-based transition mechanisms are also valuable in provider edge (PE) to customer edge (CE) scenarios, especially in service provider environments offering IPv6 connectivity to customers over an IPv4 MPLS core. In such designs, GRE tunnels are created between PE and CE routers, allowing IPv6 packets to traverse the IPv4 MPLS network without requiring native IPv6 support within the core. This tunneling model maintains address family separation, simplifies control plane operation, and enables scalable deployment of IPv6 services without disrupting existing IPv4 services. Additionally, GRE tunnels can be configured with quality of service policies, encryption, and monitoring, providing the same level of service assurance for IPv6 traffic as for traditional IPv4.

Security considerations must be addressed when deploying GRE for IPv6 transition. Since GRE lacks built-in encryption or authentication, it is often used in conjunction with IPsec to protect the encapsulated IPv6 traffic. This is especially important when tunnels traverse untrusted or public networks. GRE over IPsec ensures confidentiality, integrity, and authenticity while enabling the transport of IPv6 packets across existing IPv4 internet connections. In such cases, IPsec policies are configured to protect the GRE tunnel endpoints, and the inner IPv6 packets are secured against eavesdropping and tampering. This layered approach allows organizations to meet security requirements while continuing the migration toward IPv6.

Performance and operational considerations are also central to using GRE in transition mechanisms. GRE encapsulation adds additional headers to each packet, which increases the packet size and reduces the effective Maximum Transmission Unit (MTU). If not properly accounted for, this can lead to fragmentation or packet loss, especially in networks with strict MTU constraints. Administrators must configure appropriate MTU and MSS settings on tunnel interfaces and ensure that path MTU discovery functions correctly. Performance monitoring tools must also be aware of GRE tunnels and capable of tracking encapsulated traffic to diagnose issues such as latency, jitter, or throughput degradation.

Automation and orchestration play a growing role in the deployment of GRE tunnels for IPv6 transition. As networks scale, manually configuring GRE tunnels becomes impractical. Tools such as Ansible, Terraform, and vendor-specific SDN controllers can automate tunnel creation, manage routing configuration, and apply security policies across the transition infrastructure. This ensures consistency, reduces human error, and enables rapid adaptation as network demands evolve. In multi-cloud and hybrid environments, automated GRE deployment allows administrators to bridge IPv6 and IPv4 domains across diverse platforms and geographies, accelerating the transition process.

In enterprise environments, GRE supports internal IPv6 migration by enabling isolated segments to communicate before a full network-wide transition is achieved. Departments or locations that adopt IPv6 earlier can use GRE to connect with legacy IPv4 systems or to reach external IPv6 services via IPv4 gateways. This capability allows for phased migration, pilot testing, and compatibility verification without disrupting ongoing business operations. GRE tunnels can also support temporary connections during the transition phase, allowing engineers to validate IPv6 behavior and refine configurations before committing to permanent changes.

GRE remains one of the most effective tools in the IPv6 transition toolkit, providing protocol-agnostic tunneling that supports both IPv6-over-IPv4 and IPv4-over-IPv6 scenarios. Its flexibility, compatibility with existing routing protocols, and support for security extensions make it a reliable choice for network architects navigating the complex shift to IPv6. As organizations continue to embrace IPv6 to meet the demands of a growing internet and increasing address exhaustion, GRE will continue to serve as a vital mechanism for ensuring interoperability, stability, and forward compatibility in the ever-evolving world of network communication.

Use Cases for Nested GRE Tunnels

Nested GRE tunnels represent a more advanced use of Generic Routing Encapsulation technology in which one GRE tunnel is encapsulated within another. While standard GRE tunnels are used widely for connecting networks, enabling routing adjacencies, or transporting multicast and non-IP protocols, nesting adds a layer of complexity and flexibility that can be leveraged for specialized use cases. By encapsulating a GRE tunnel within another GRE tunnel, network architects can create multiple levels of isolation, support hierarchical routing, implement traffic engineering solutions, and satisfy layered policy or security requirements. Although this approach introduces additional encapsulation overhead and complexity, it unlocks capabilities that are particularly useful in environments where separation, multi-tenancy, or transport abstraction is required.

One of the most prominent use cases for nested GRE tunnels is multi-tenant network design. In large enterprise or service provider environments where multiple customers or departments share the same physical infrastructure, ensuring strict traffic segregation is critical. The outer GRE tunnel can be used to represent the physical transport layer, possibly between data centers or across an MPLS backbone, while the inner GRE tunnel encapsulates tenant-specific traffic. This dual-layer model allows the provider to use a shared underlay for efficient resource utilization while maintaining completely isolated logical topologies for each tenant. Each tenant's inner GRE tunnel can have its own routing, encryption policies, and even traffic engineering mechanisms, enabling tailored services without compromising security or performance.

Another significant application of nested GRE is for secure overlays across public or untrusted networks. In scenarios where a GRE tunnel must pass through multiple administrative domains, or across public infrastructure like the Internet, encapsulating the GRE tunnel inside another GRE or IPsec-protected tunnel can provide an extra layer of policy enforcement or encryption. For example, the outer GRE tunnel may be protected with IPsec to secure the overall transport path, while the inner GRE tunnel can facilitate dynamic routing between internal routers or carry application-specific traffic. This structure allows organizations to maintain internal routing control and service chaining, even when the outer path is traversing unknown or untrusted infrastructure.

Nested GRE tunnels are also useful in simulation and testing environments where complex, layered topologies need to be emulated without the physical infrastructure to support them. Network engineers and software developers often create nested GRE topologies to test failover logic, routing protocol behavior, or multi-hop security policies. By nesting tunnels, they can simulate multiple logical paths, different administrative domains, and layered network services within a single lab environment. This is particularly valuable in the development of SD-WAN, cloud networking, or virtual network function platforms where full production-like environments must be replicated for testing purposes without replicating all the hardware.

In advanced routing scenarios, nested GRE enables the separation of control and data planes, allowing different routing domains to coexist and interoperate. The outer tunnel might carry control plane traffic between two SDN controllers or orchestrators, while the inner tunnel is responsible for forwarding user traffic between edge devices. This distinction allows for granular policy application and operational visibility into each layer of traffic. It also supports troubleshooting and analytics by allowing network monitoring tools to differentiate between infrastructure control messages and application flows.

Nested GRE tunnels can also be used in disaster recovery and high-availability scenarios. Organizations often need to replicate data between primary and backup sites in a way that ensures data integrity, minimizes latency, and preserves network architecture. A nested GRE model can be designed where the outer tunnel provides the path between geographic locations and the inner tunnel encapsulates sensitive replication traffic that may require additional classification, tagging, or QoS treatment. By structuring the tunnels this way, administrators can apply specific routing or failover mechanisms to each layer independently, optimizing the data path without affecting other services running on the same infrastructure.

In hybrid cloud and multi-cloud environments, nested GRE enables unified routing across different cloud providers while preserving internal security and routing structures. A GRE tunnel may be established between an enterprise data center and a cloud provider to serve as the outer transport. Within that, additional GRE tunnels can be created for each workload, service, or business unit to ensure policy consistency and secure segmentation. This model allows enterprises to abstract the complexity of the underlying cloud infrastructure and apply centralized routing, logging, and policy controls. Additionally, because each nested tunnel can be monitored and managed separately, troubleshooting and compliance enforcement become more manageable.

Network function virtualization platforms often leverage nested GRE as part of their service chaining architecture. A virtual router, firewall, or load balancer may establish inner GRE tunnels to other services in the chain, while the outer GRE tunnel manages communication between virtualized infrastructure hosts. This architecture provides clear separation between the service plane and the infrastructure plane, which is essential for scaling virtual services, applying security policies, and maintaining modularity. It allows each service to operate as an independent entity while benefiting from a shared transport mechanism, promoting operational agility and simplified lifecycle management.

When combined with Quality of Service policies, nested GRE can enforce differentiated treatment of traffic within and across tunnels. An outer GRE tunnel may be subject to a global QoS policy based on bandwidth agreements or provider constraints, while inner tunnels can carry traffic classes with distinct latency, priority, or drop policies. This allows fine-tuned control of how different types of traffic are handled, both within the organization and across third-party networks. It also supports SLA enforcement in managed service environments, where service providers must guarantee performance for multiple classes of traffic simultaneously.

While the use of nested GRE tunnels brings undeniable advantages in terms of flexibility and segmentation, it is not without challenges. Each layer of encapsulation adds header overhead, potentially impacting MTU and causing fragmentation if not managed properly. Network engineers must carefully configure MTU and MSS values and validate path MTU discovery across all tunnel hops. Troubleshooting also becomes more complex, as identifying the source of an issue may require unpacking multiple layers of encapsulation. Monitoring tools must be GRE-aware and capable of analyzing nested encapsulated packets to provide actionable insights into performance and security.

Despite these challenges, nested GRE tunnels remain a powerful solution for a range of advanced networking problems. From supporting multi-tenant services to enabling secure cloud interconnectivity and facilitating complex lab simulations, nested GRE offers capabilities that standard tunneling methods cannot match. Its ability to provide logical separation, flexible transport, and scalable service chaining makes it a valuable asset for modern networks that must accommodate growth, complexity, and evolving operational requirements. By understanding the use cases and managing the operational implications, network architects can harness the full potential of nested GRE tunnels to build intelligent, modular, and resilient network architectures.

Advanced GRE Debugging Techniques

Generic Routing Encapsulation, or GRE, is a fundamental tunneling protocol used in many enterprise and service provider networks to encapsulate Layer 3 traffic across IP networks. Its simplicity and protocol agnosticism make it ideal for carrying a wide range of traffic types, including multicast, IPv6, and routing protocol updates. However, when GRE tunnels do not function as expected, diagnosing the issue requires a structured, methodical approach. Unlike protocols with built-in session management and state tracking, GRE's stateless nature can complicate troubleshooting, especially when multiple tunnels are deployed across various routing domains or when tunnels traverse complex topologies with NAT, firewalls, or QoS mechanisms. Advanced GRE debugging techniques involve the use of interface diagnostics, routing verification, packet captures, encapsulation analysis, and performance monitoring to isolate and resolve issues efficiently.

A critical first step in GRE tunnel troubleshooting is verifying the logical and physical status of the tunnel interface. On most platforms, the tunnel interface appears as a virtual interface that can be monitored using standard show commands. The line protocol status must be examined closely, as it typically reflects the reachability of the tunnel destination. If the tunnel interface is down, it is essential to confirm that the tunnel source and destination addresses are correct and reachable via the routing table. Recursive routing issues are a frequent source of GRE tunnel failures, where the route to the tunnel destination points back into the tunnel itself, creating a loop that prevents proper resolution. Verifying that the tunnel destination is reachable through a non-tunneled path and checking the administrative distance and metrics of associated routes are essential tasks during the initial stages of debugging.

Packet capture and analysis are indispensable for advanced GRE troubleshooting. Capturing traffic on both the source and destination interfaces allows engineers to confirm whether GRE packets are being sent and received. The GRE header includes fields such as protocol type, checksum, and key values that can be inspected to verify the integrity and configuration of the tunnel. Tools like Wireshark or tcpdump can decode GRE encapsulated packets and help identify anomalies such as incorrect protocol types or malformed headers. In environments where multiple tunnels exist, using GRE key fields to differentiate between tunnels becomes crucial. GRE keys are optional identifiers that can be configured to allow classification of encapsulated traffic, particularly in environments where load balancing or multi-tenant separation is required. Misconfigured or mismatched GRE keys on the tunnel endpoints often result in dropped packets or traffic reaching the wrong destination, a problem that can be detected through header inspection in packet captures.

Verifying encapsulated routing protocol behavior is another layer of GRE debugging. Many GRE tunnels are used specifically to transport dynamic routing updates, such as OSPF, EIGRP, or BGP. If these routing protocols fail to establish adjacencies across the tunnel, the issue may lie in MTU mismatches, ACLs blocking protocol traffic, or inconsistent tunnel policies. Capturing routing protocol packets as they traverse the GRE tunnel allows engineers to determine whether hello packets are being sent and whether acknowledgments or updates are being received. Analyzing the source and destination IPs of these packets ensures they match expected values, while reviewing TTL, flags, and checksum values helps diagnose protocol-specific issues. If routing adjacencies are not forming, verifying the correct network types, timers, and authentication parameters on both ends of the tunnel becomes necessary.

MTU and fragmentation issues frequently surface in GRE environments due to the additional header overhead that GRE adds to each packet. GRE encapsulation increases packet size, and if the resulting packets exceed the physical interface MTU, they may be dropped or fragmented. This can lead to performance degradation, session instability, or outright communication failures for certain applications. Advanced debugging techniques involve enabling Path MTU Discovery and monitoring ICMP fragmentation-needed messages to ensure that intermediate devices are not silently discarding oversized packets. Additionally, configuring the TCP MSS (Maximum Segment Size) on the GRE tunnel interface helps prevent fragmentation by limiting the size of packets at the transport layer. Observing flow behaviors under load and capturing traffic during application usage can highlight if and where fragmentation is occurring, and whether it is being handled gracefully by the network.

Another advanced diagnostic approach involves checking the performance and error counters on the GRE tunnel interface. Many routers maintain detailed interface statistics that reveal packet drops, input errors, output errors, and other anomalies. A rising count of input errors might indicate malformed GRE packets, unsupported encapsulation options, or checksum errors. Output drops may suggest queue congestion or a misbehaving routing protocol injecting excessive traffic into the tunnel. Monitoring tools that poll SNMP counters or collect telemetry data can provide continuous visibility into these metrics and help correlate tunnel performance with network events.

Security features such as firewalls, access control lists, and intrusion prevention systems can also impact GRE tunnel functionality. Firewalls may block IP protocol 47, which is used by GRE, or may perform deep packet inspection that misinterprets GRE encapsulated packets as anomalous traffic. When tunnels traverse firewalls, it is essential to confirm that GRE is explicitly allowed and that any NAT translation does not interfere with GRE headers. In some advanced firewalls, GRE sessions can be tracked using application-layer gateways or protocol helpers, but these features may require specific configurations or firmware versions. Debugging GRE through firewalls often necessitates collaboration with security teams to review firewall logs, policy matches, and packet traces.

QoS mechanisms must also be evaluated during GRE debugging. When traffic is encapsulated within GRE, QoS markings such as DSCP may not be preserved or interpreted correctly unless explicitly configured. Some routers support DSCP transparency or remarking features that ensure the inner packet's QoS values are copied to the outer GRE header, allowing intermediate devices to apply proper queuing and shaping policies. Analyzing whether QoS policies are being applied as expected requires examining both the GRE encapsulated packets and the resulting forwarding behavior across the network. Tools like IP SLA and performance probes can simulate traffic over the tunnel and report on latency, jitter, and loss, helping to pinpoint where QoS misconfigurations may be impacting GRE tunnel traffic.

Debugging GRE tunnels at scale introduces additional complexities, especially in networks with dynamic tunnel creation, such as those found in SD-WAN or cloud-based platforms. Automation tools that deploy GRE tunnels programmatically may introduce errors if templates are misconfigured or parameters are inconsistent across nodes. Logging and audit trails from configuration management systems become valuable sources of information when tracing the history of tunnel configuration changes. In such environments, centralized monitoring systems that track tunnel creation, status, and performance in real-time are essential for rapid identification and resolution of issues.

GRE debugging is both an art and a science, requiring a comprehensive understanding of the protocol's behavior, a meticulous approach to isolating variables, and the effective use of diagnostic tools. Whether resolving a single broken tunnel or evaluating the health of dozens across a distributed network, the techniques described provide the foundational skills necessary to maintain stable and efficient GRE-based connectivity.

Packet Capture in GRE Tunnels

Packet capture in GRE tunnels is one of the most critical diagnostic and analysis techniques available to network engineers and administrators. GRE, or Generic Routing Encapsulation, is a protocol used to encapsulate a wide variety of Layer 3 protocols within IP tunnels, enabling point-to-point communication over otherwise incompatible networks. While GRE provides flexible transport for unicast, multicast, IPv6, and routing protocol traffic, it also introduces complexity when troubleshooting, monitoring, or auditing the traffic that flows through these tunnels. To understand what is happening inside a GRE tunnel, one must go beyond standard packet capture methodologies and apply targeted techniques that allow visibility into both the outer encapsulation and the encapsulated payload.

The fundamental concept of a GRE tunnel is simple: take an original IP packet and encapsulate it with a new GRE header and a new outer IP header. The outer header provides the addressing required for the packet to traverse the physical or logical network path between GRE endpoints, while the inner payload remains unchanged and is only interpreted by the destination tunnel endpoint. This encapsulation makes GRE extremely useful for scenarios like VPNs, routing protocol adjacencies across noncontiguous segments, and protocol bridging. However, this same encapsulation means that traditional packet capture performed at intermediary points between the GRE source and destination only shows the outer GRE-encapsulated packets. These observers are blind to the actual payload unless decapsulation is performed during analysis.

Performing packet capture at the GRE tunnel source or destination allows a full view of both the original packet before encapsulation and the resulting GRE-encapsulated frame. When the capture point is inside the router or firewall creating the GRE tunnel, the original packet can be seen on the ingress interface, followed by the GRE-encapsulated version on the egress interface. Conversely, at the destination tunnel endpoint, the GRE packet is received on the ingress interface and decapsulated, producing the original packet on the egress interface. Capturing both directions provides a complete picture of how packets are handled and modified by the tunneling process, which is essential for verifying correct operation and troubleshooting communication problems.

Tools such as Wireshark, tcpdump, and vendor-specific diagnostic utilities are indispensable for performing these captures. Wireshark, for example, has built-in support for decoding GRE headers and parsing the encapsulated packet, making it easier to analyze complex tunneling scenarios. When capturing GRE traffic, filters must be applied carefully to focus on the correct protocol and address pairings. For instance, GRE uses IP protocol number 47, so filters based on this value can isolate GRE traffic from the broader stream of IP packets. Additionally, filtering by the source and destination IP addresses of the GRE endpoints helps narrow the scope of the capture and exclude unrelated traffic.

One of the most valuable features in GRE packet analysis is the ability to inspect the encapsulated payload. Once GRE packets are captured, modern tools allow for recursive protocol decoding, displaying the inner IP packet and any associated transport layer data. This is critical for determining whether the encapsulated traffic is correct, whether packet fragmentation is occurring, and whether routing or application-layer issues exist within the tunnel. It also helps identify misconfigurations such as GRE key mismatches, incorrect encapsulation types, or tunnel loop conditions. If the encapsulated packet is malformed or incomplete, it may indicate an issue in the encapsulation logic at the source or a problem with MTU handling along the tunnel path.

In many networks, GRE tunnels coexist with multiple types of traffic, and multiple tunnels may operate simultaneously between the same endpoints. In such environments, GRE key fields can be used to differentiate between logical tunnels within a single physical path. When configured, GRE keys are inserted into the GRE header and can be captured and analyzed to confirm proper tunnel identification. This is particularly useful in multi-tenant scenarios or in advanced routing configurations where different services or clients are assigned separate logical tunnels. Packet capture tools that support GRE key field decoding allow analysts to verify that packets are being assigned to the correct tunnel and to detect any cross-tunnel leakage or misrouting.

Packet capture within GRE tunnels also enables in-depth performance monitoring and SLA validation. By examining timestamps, sequence numbers, and application-layer headers within the encapsulated packets, administrators can measure latency, jitter, and throughput across the GRE tunnel. This analysis is essential for understanding the impact of GRE encapsulation on real-time applications such as voice or video and for validating that QoS policies are being enforced correctly. Captures can reveal whether DSCP values are being preserved, altered, or stripped during encapsulation, and whether shaping, policing, or queuing behaviors are having the intended effect on the tunneled traffic.

In environments where GRE tunnels traverse NAT devices, firewalls, or load balancers, packet capture becomes even more critical. These middleboxes can alter packet headers, block GRE protocol 47, or perform translation that disrupts the tunnel. Capturing traffic on both sides of the NAT or firewall allows for comparative analysis to determine whether packets are being modified or dropped. It can also expose issues such as asymmetrical routing, incorrect security policy enforcement, or TTL expiration. This visibility is vital for confirming that the GRE tunnel is being allowed through these devices and that no hidden policy or inspection feature is interfering with traffic flow.

Capturing packets in encrypted GRE tunnels adds additional complexity. When GRE is used over IPsec, the outer packet is encrypted, making it impossible to analyze the encapsulated data without decrypting the IPsec payload. In such cases, capturing traffic before encryption (on the GRE interface) and after decryption (at the tunnel endpoint) provides the necessary visibility. Analysts must understand where in the packet flow to capture data to obtain useful insights. Capturing post-IPsec means seeing the GRE encapsulated packets, which can then be analyzed as in any unencrypted scenario.

In contrast, capturing pre-IPsec or inside the tunnel allows access to the clear-text payload.

Storage and filtering of GRE capture data should also be managed carefully. GRE tunnels can generate significant traffic, especially in data center or backbone environments. Captures should be time-limited, focused on specific IP pairs or ports, and stored with sufficient metadata to allow for accurate post-analysis. Automated systems can be configured to trigger captures based on tunnel status changes, traffic anomalies, or predefined SLA violations. This automation enables proactive diagnostics and faster resolution of performance or connectivity issues.

Overall, packet capture in GRE tunnels is not just a troubleshooting tool but a strategic capability for managing modern IP networks. It allows engineers to peel back the layers of encapsulation and see the actual traffic being transported, revealing issues that are otherwise invisible to conventional monitoring. Whether used for debugging, performance tuning, or security verification, packet analysis of GRE traffic provides the granularity and clarity necessary to ensure that GRE tunnels perform reliably, securely, and in accordance with design intent. With proper tools, techniques, and a methodical approach, network professionals can harness the full diagnostic power of packet capture to maintain and optimize GRE-based communication.

GRE Tunnel Design Best Practices

Designing GRE tunnels for enterprise or service provider networks involves far more than simply configuring source and destination IP addresses and enabling the tunnel interface. While the configuration itself may appear straightforward, the underlying network architecture, traffic characteristics, routing strategies, and security considerations all influence the effectiveness, stability, and scalability of the GRE implementation. GRE, or Generic Routing Encapsulation, is a flexible, lightweight tunneling protocol capable of encapsulating a wide range of Layer 3 protocols. Its versatility makes it a popular choice for bridging disparate networks, enabling dynamic routing adjacencies across non-contiguous topologies, and transporting multicast or IPv6 traffic over legacy infrastructure. However, without adherence to established best practices in tunnel design, GRE deployments can introduce operational challenges such as routing loops, traffic black-holing, performance degradation, and security vulnerabilities.

One of the most critical best practices in GRE tunnel design is avoiding recursive routing dependencies. GRE tunnels rely on the underlying routing table to resolve the destination IP address of the remote tunnel endpoint. If the route to the tunnel destination is learned through the tunnel itself, a recursive dependency is created. This can result in a routing loop where the packet continuously tries to reach its destination through the tunnel, which cannot be established because the tunnel's reachability depends on the very path it is supposed to build. The route to the GRE destination must be reachable through a physical or logical path that exists independently of the tunnel interface. Designing clear and separate control paths for tunnel reachability ensures that tunnels are built on stable underlay networks and that failover scenarios do not result in recursive failure.

Selecting appropriate tunnel source and destination IP addresses also contributes to robust GRE tunnel design. These addresses should be statically assigned and ideally reside on loopback interfaces or interfaces with high availability configurations such as port channels or VRRP-enabled links. Using loopback interfaces provides stability, as these interfaces do not go down unless the entire router fails. This design decision enhances routing protocol resilience, improves tunnel stability, and supports consistent peer relationships in the event of physical interface failover. Additionally, the use of routable, globally unique IP addresses for GRE endpoints ensures that tunnel traffic can traverse complex topologies, including NAT, without ambiguity or translation conflicts.

MTU and fragmentation handling must be factored into the tunnel design from the beginning. GRE adds overhead to each encapsulated packet, and when this additional header size causes the packet to exceed the path MTU, fragmentation can occur. Excessive fragmentation leads to increased latency, potential packet loss, and poor application performance, particularly for real-time traffic. Tunnel interfaces should be configured with appropriate MTU values, accounting for the GRE and IP headers. Path MTU Discovery should be enabled whenever possible to allow endpoints to learn the optimal packet size dynamically. Additionally, setting the TCP MSS (Maximum Segment Size) on tunnel interfaces helps avoid fragmentation by limiting packet size at the transport layer, which ensures consistent and reliable data transmission.

Traffic engineering is another key element in GRE tunnel design. Tunnels can be used to implement overlay networks, support redundant paths, or provide route segmentation. When multiple GRE tunnels exist between sites, equal-cost multipath (ECMP) routing can be used to distribute traffic. However, this requires careful alignment of routing metrics, tunnel interface configurations, and hash algorithms used for load balancing. Designers should determine whether per-packet or per-flow load balancing is appropriate for the traffic profile and confirm that all devices in the path support the required ECMP behavior. In scenarios requiring primary and backup tunnels, routing protocols should be configured with metric offsets or administrative distances to enforce the preferred path. Tunnel tracking mechanisms such as GRE keepalives or BFD (Bidirectional Forwarding Detection) can enhance failover responsiveness by detecting tunnel outages more quickly than standard routing protocol timers.

Security must also be considered in GRE tunnel design, especially when tunnels traverse untrusted networks. GRE by itself does not provide encryption, authentication, or integrity checking. To secure GRE traffic, tunnels should be encapsulated within IPsec to create GRE-over-IPsec configurations. This approach protects the encapsulated payload from eavesdropping, tampering, and spoofing. The IPsec policies must be carefully designed to match the tunnel source and destination, and security associations should be monitored and managed to ensure reliable operation. For additional granularity, GRE key fields can be used to identify specific tunnels or traffic types, adding a logical identifier that helps enforce policy and maintain traffic segregation.

Operational visibility and monitoring are essential components of effective GRE tunnel deployment. Tunnel interfaces should be included in the network monitoring platform to track status, throughput, error rates, and protocol health. SNMP-based tools, flow exporters, and telemetry streams can provide insights into tunnel utilization and performance trends, enabling proactive troubleshooting and capacity planning. Logging and alerting should be configured to capture tunnel state changes, including flapping, keepalive failures, and route withdrawal events. In multi-site or high-scale environments, automated validation and testing of GRE tunnel functionality become critical. Scripts or orchestration tools can periodically test tunnel reachability, measure latency, and verify that routing protocols are maintaining stable adjacencies.

In virtualized and cloud environments, GRE tunnels must be designed with awareness of the hypervisor, overlay network, and virtual routing fabric. When GRE endpoints are virtual machines or containers, their network interfaces must be connected to virtual switches that support the required encapsulation and performance characteristics. Performance tuning, such as enabling hardware offload of tunnel processing or allocating sufficient CPU resources to virtual routers, helps maintain throughput and low latency. Cloud deployments may involve GRE tunnels across regions or providers, requiring additional attention to underlay routing, MTU differences, and firewall or NAT traversal. GRE-over-IPsec remains a preferred method for securely connecting cloud-hosted resources to on-premises networks when native VPN services do not support the required routing flexibility.

GRE tunnels are often used as part of larger architectures involving MPLS, VRF segmentation, or SD-WAN overlays. In these scenarios, tunnel design must align with the broader network policy and topology. For example, GRE tunnels between VRF instances must ensure correct binding and route leaking rules to preserve traffic isolation. Similarly, when integrating GRE with MPLS, label distribution and path selection mechanisms must be coordinated with the encapsulated traffic patterns. GRE tunnels can serve as transport underlays or logical overlays depending on the design model, and the role they play determines how routing, QoS, and security policies are applied.

By adhering to these best practices in GRE tunnel design, network architects can build resilient, efficient, and secure networks that meet the demands of modern applications and services. Whether used for extending routing domains, connecting hybrid clouds, enabling disaster recovery, or supporting segmented overlays, GRE remains a powerful tool—when designed with precision and aligned to operational goals. The balance between simplicity and sophistication lies in the understanding of tunnel behavior across all layers of the network, from routing and encapsulation to security and performance monitoring. Through meticulous planning and continuous validation, GRE tunnels can deliver the agility and control required in dynamic, multi-domain network environments.

Migration Strategies to GRE

Migrating a network infrastructure to incorporate Generic Routing Encapsulation, or GRE, requires careful planning, phased execution, and comprehensive validation to ensure a seamless transition from legacy connectivity models. GRE is a versatile tunneling protocol that enables the encapsulation of a wide range of network layer protocols within IP tunnels, creating virtual point-to-point links over an existing IP network. This capability is valuable for unifying disparate network segments, supporting routing protocol adjacencies across noncontiguous domains, and extending networks across public or private infrastructure without altering core configurations. The migration to GRE becomes necessary when organizations seek to modernize their networks, support hybrid architectures, or simplify routing complexity by abstracting physical topology. However, implementing GRE into an operational environment without causing disruption demands a structured strategy that considers the unique challenges of each deployment scenario.

The initial phase in migrating to GRE involves evaluating the current network topology and identifying the segments that will benefit most from GRE tunnels. These may include branch locations, remote offices, data centers, or cloud environments that require secure and predictable communication paths. The assessment must include the existing routing protocol infrastructure, addressing schemes, firewall and NAT policies, and the availability of devices that support GRE natively. This discovery phase lays the foundation for designing a GRE overlay that complements rather than disrupts the underlay network. It is also during this stage that performance requirements, security needs, and failover considerations are defined to guide the configuration of the GRE tunnels.

A migration to GRE is typically executed in a phased manner, beginning with pilot deployments. Pilot sites are selected based on their strategic importance, manageable complexity, and willingness to participate in the testing process. These sites are connected using GRE tunnels established between their local edge routers and a central aggregation point. During this phase, routing adjacency over GRE is configured, connectivity is verified, and performance is monitored. Any issues uncovered during the pilot, such as routing loops, MTU mismatches, or encapsulation errors, are resolved before scaling the deployment. This phase acts as a proof of concept and provides the operational teams with the necessary experience to handle broader rollouts.

Routing migration must be approached with caution to avoid disrupting established forwarding paths. In networks using dynamic routing protocols like OSPF, EIGRP, or BGP, careful manipulation of route metrics and redistribution policies ensures a non-disruptive shift in path preference. GRE tunnels should initially be introduced as backup paths with higher administrative distance or cost, allowing operators to verify their stability and performance before making them the primary route. Once validated, route preferences can be adjusted to favor the GRE tunnel, gradually transitioning traffic while maintaining fallback options. This staged routing cutover provides continuity of service and avoids abrupt traffic shifts that might impact users or applications.

Firewall and NAT configurations are another critical aspect of GRE migration. Since GRE operates as IP protocol number 47 and not over TCP or UDP, firewalls must be explicitly configured to allow GRE traffic. NAT traversal is particularly challenging, as most NAT devices do not handle GRE without special configuration. During the migration, administrators must ensure that GRE passthrough is enabled on firewalls or consider tunneling GRE inside IPsec or UDP wrappers to facilitate traversal. Failing to configure security policies to accommodate GRE will result in dropped packets and failed tunnel establishment. Early validation of firewall behavior and NAT compatibility reduces the likelihood of encountering these issues during the wider rollout.

To address performance and overhead, migration strategies should include a review of MTU settings and potential fragmentation issues. Since GRE encapsulation adds additional headers, packets may exceed the standard MTU, resulting in fragmentation unless adjustments are made. MTU values on tunnel interfaces must be set appropriately, and TCP MSS clamping should be configured to prevent oversized packets. Path MTU discovery mechanisms should be tested to ensure that they function correctly in the presence of GRE. These adjustments are essential for maintaining performance, especially for latency-sensitive applications like voice or video, which can suffer from poor performance when encapsulation-induced fragmentation is not properly managed.

In organizations with strict security policies, GRE migration must include the integration of encryption and authentication mechanisms. GRE does not provide inherent encryption, so when tunnels traverse untrusted networks, they must be encapsulated within IPsec. GRE-over-IPsec configurations allow organizations to preserve GRE's routing and protocol flexibility while meeting security compliance requirements. During the migration, establishing the IPsec framework alongside GRE tunnel deployment ensures that no data traverses the network without appropriate protection. Key exchange mechanisms, IPsec policies, and certificate management processes must be validated and documented during the pilot phase to avoid issues during full-scale deployment.

As the migration progresses, automation and orchestration tools become increasingly valuable. Manually configuring tunnels across dozens or hundreds of endpoints introduces the risk of human error and inconsistency. Configuration management tools such as Ansible or vendor-specific orchestration platforms can automate tunnel creation, routing policy updates, and monitoring configuration. Templates can be defined for different site roles, ensuring uniform deployment across the network. This automation accelerates migration, enhances consistency, and allows for rapid rollback if issues are encountered. Real-time monitoring and logging must also be implemented to track the performance and health of GRE tunnels. Metrics such as tunnel uptime, packet loss, latency, and jitter provide critical insight into tunnel stability and help identify problem areas before they impact users.

Training and documentation are essential components of the GRE migration strategy. Network engineers and support staff must be educated on GRE tunnel behavior, troubleshooting techniques, and operational best practices. Documentation must include tunnel topology diagrams, configuration templates, routing policies, firewall rules, and security profiles. This knowledge base supports ongoing operations and reduces reliance on a small group of experts. It also facilitates future expansion or changes to the GRE overlay, enabling the organization to respond quickly to business demands.

Post-migration validation ensures that the GRE tunnels are delivering on their intended purpose. Functional tests should verify reachability, routing convergence, and failover behavior. Application performance should be evaluated to ensure that the GRE tunnel is not introducing unacceptable delays or instability. In the case of hybrid networks, where GRE connects on-premises infrastructure with cloud resources, connectivity to cloud services, load balancers, and virtual appliances must be verified under load. Feedback from users and application owners should be collected to confirm that the migration has had no negative impact and to gather input for future improvements.

By carefully planning, testing, and executing each phase of the GRE migration process, organizations can modernize their network architecture, introduce scalable overlay connectivity, and support complex routing needs without sacrificing performance or security. GRE becomes a reliable foundation for routing flexibility, hybrid cloud interconnection, and multi-site communication when deployed with precision and guided by strategic migration principles.

GRE and Compliance Requirements

Generic Routing Encapsulation, or GRE, is a protocol widely used for tunneling various Layer 3 traffic types across IP networks. Its primary strength lies in its flexibility, allowing the encapsulation of different protocols such as IPv6, multicast, and even routing updates over an existing IP infrastructure. While GRE is often deployed to extend routing domains, connect isolated network segments, and enable dynamic overlay topologies, its usage introduces several implications when it comes to compliance requirements in regulated industries. Organizations operating in sectors such as finance, healthcare, defense, and critical infrastructure must adhere to stringent data protection, confidentiality, integrity, and accountability standards. Therefore, the deployment and management of GRE tunnels must be evaluated not only from a technical perspective but also from a regulatory one.

One of the most pressing compliance concerns related to GRE is the lack of native encryption or authentication. GRE encapsulates data packets but does not secure them. This means that any packet traveling through a GRE tunnel is vulnerable to interception, tampering, and replay if it traverses an untrusted network. For organizations subject to compliance frameworks such as HIPAA, PCI DSS, GDPR, or FISMA, unencrypted transmission of sensitive data violates core mandates. These standards typically require that data in transit be protected using strong encryption and secure authentication methods. As GRE alone does not provide such protections, it must be paired with additional protocols like IPsec to meet compliance requirements. GRE-over-IPsec is the most common method for ensuring that tunneled traffic remains confidential and tamper-proof. In such configurations, GRE handles the encapsulation of Layer 3 traffic, while IPsec encrypts the entire GRE payload, thus meeting encryption and integrity standards required by regulatory bodies.

Beyond encryption, compliance requirements often include strict access control and segmentation mandates. Frameworks like ISO 27001 and NIST SP 800-53 specify the need to isolate data flows between environments with different sensitivity levels. GRE tunnels must be carefully designed to prevent unauthorized access or traffic leakage between segments. This involves binding GRE tunnels to specific routing domains, implementing GRE key fields to differentiate logical connections, and using virtual routing and forwarding (VRF) instances to maintain traffic segregation. Any misconfiguration that allows GRE traffic from one segment to reach another without authorization could be interpreted as a compliance violation, leading to fines or operational restrictions. Therefore, a policy-driven approach to GRE configuration must be implemented, supported by detailed documentation and validation processes.

Logging and monitoring are also critical compliance requirements that apply to GRE tunnel operations. Regulations often mandate that all access to protected systems and data must be logged and that these logs must be retained for specific durations, typically ranging from 90 days to several years. However, GRE traffic can obscure the true origin and nature of encapsulated packets, making traditional monitoring tools insufficient. To remain compliant, organizations must deploy monitoring systems capable of inspecting GRE tunnels at the ingress and egress points. These systems must log tunnel establishment and teardown events, changes in tunnel status, unusual traffic patterns, and anomalies such as packet drops or high latency. In environments where GRE tunnels are encrypted with IPsec, compliance still demands metadata tracking and endpoint accountability, even if payload inspection is limited. All collected logs should be time-synchronized and stored in tamper-proof repositories, supporting forensic analysis and audit trail requirements.

Data residency and sovereignty requirements present another compliance challenge for GRE tunnel deployments. Certain regulations, such as those found in GDPR and regional cybersecurity laws, dictate that specific types of data must remain within defined geographic boundaries. When GRE tunnels span across regions or countries, especially over the public internet or third-party provider infrastructure, organizations must ensure that sensitive data is not inadvertently routed through or terminated in noncompliant jurisdictions. This necessitates the use of geo-fencing and traffic routing policies that control where GRE tunnels are established and how traffic flows between endpoints. In some cases, compliance may require that tunnels use dedicated private infrastructure or that additional controls, such as localized data encryption keys or endpoint certification, be implemented to satisfy jurisdictional mandates.

Compliance frameworks also call for vulnerability management and periodic assessments of all systems that handle sensitive data. GRE tunnels must be included in these evaluations, with regular testing to ensure that no tunnel is misconfigured, exposed, or susceptible to known threats such as spoofing or denial-of-service attacks. Penetration testing and vulnerability scanning should validate that tunnel endpoints are properly hardened, that GRE packets cannot be injected by unauthorized sources, and that IPsec configurations meet the minimum cryptographic standards set by the regulatory body in question. Any deficiencies discovered must be remediated within the timeline dictated by the applicable framework, and records of the findings and fixes must be documented for audit purposes.

Change management is another compliance-related consideration in GRE tunnel design and maintenance. All changes to GRE tunnel configurations, including endpoint updates, routing modifications, or encryption policy alterations, must be logged and follow a formal change control process. This includes authorization workflows, impact assessments, rollback plans, and change documentation. In regulated environments, unapproved or undocumented changes can lead to audit findings and compliance breaches. Automation tools used to manage GRE configurations must integrate with change control systems, and configuration backups must be taken regularly to ensure that the state of the GRE infrastructure can be restored in case of failure or compromise.

Employee access and administrative control over GRE tunnel configurations are also scrutinized under compliance standards. Only authorized personnel should be able to create, modify, or delete GRE tunnels. Role-based access control (RBAC), two-factor authentication, and privilege auditing should be implemented on systems managing GRE infrastructure. Credentials used for accessing tunnel endpoints must be rotated regularly and protected using secure vaults. Any misuse or unauthorized access attempts must trigger alerts and be investigated promptly. This level of control and oversight is vital for compliance with standards that mandate strict accountability for administrative actions and configuration changes.

GRE tunnels must also be evaluated in the context of data classification. Not all traffic encapsulated within a GRE tunnel is equally sensitive. However, compliance requirements often treat tunneled data as high risk because of the potential for carrying unauthorized or unmonitored traffic. As a result, GRE tunnel usage policies must include traffic classification rules, access control lists, and service policies that define what types of data may be transported. GRE tunnels should not be used as general-purpose transit paths for mixed-sensitivity data unless accompanied by mechanisms that enforce policy-based separation and data handling controls.

GRE, as a tunneling technology, provides immense value in creating scalable and flexible network architectures, especially in hybrid cloud and multi-site deployments. However, its use must be aligned with a comprehensive compliance strategy that accounts for encryption, access control, monitoring, logging, segmentation, and operational governance. Without these measures, the very flexibility that makes GRE attractive can become a liability in environments where regulatory adherence is mandatory. Organizations seeking to deploy or expand GRE infrastructure must do so within a framework that treats compliance as an integral design parameter, ensuring that every tunnel not only supports operational goals but also upholds the standards that protect sensitive data, ensure transparency, and build trust with stakeholders and regulators alike.

Security Risks in GRE Tunnels

Generic Routing Encapsulation, or GRE, is a popular tunneling protocol used to encapsulate various network layer protocols inside IP packets for transmission across incompatible networks. While GRE offers considerable flexibility and is frequently used to support dynamic routing, multicast traffic, and connectivity across hybrid and segmented environments, it introduces a range of security concerns that must be thoroughly understood and addressed. Unlike protocols that provide built-in security features such as encryption, authentication, or access control, GRE is inherently insecure by design. Its lightweight and stateless architecture prioritize speed and compatibility, which makes it vulnerable to a variety of threats, particularly when deployed over untrusted networks like the public internet.

One of the most prominent security risks associated with GRE is the complete lack of encryption. GRE encapsulates data packets but does not offer any form of confidentiality. Any data transmitted through a

GRE tunnel is sent in cleartext, meaning that an attacker with access to any segment of the transmission path can intercept and read the encapsulated packets without any special tools. This is particularly dangerous when sensitive information such as usernames, passwords, financial records, or internal routing updates are sent over the tunnel. In environments that handle personally identifiable information, intellectual property, or regulatory data, the use of unencrypted GRE tunnels may violate compliance requirements and create legal exposure in the event of a data breach.

GRE tunnels are also vulnerable to spoofing attacks. Because GRE does not verify the identity of the source or the integrity of the encapsulated packet, an attacker can forge GRE packets with a valid-looking source IP address and send them to a tunnel endpoint. If the endpoint accepts the traffic without any form of authentication or validation, the attacker may be able to inject malicious data, manipulate routing tables, or initiate denial-of-service attacks. Spoofed GRE packets can disrupt legitimate communication within the tunnel, poison route advertisements, or trick endpoints into consuming resources with forged sessions or repetitive encapsulated traffic.

Another serious risk involves GRE's compatibility with recursive routing configurations, which, if misconfigured, can create routing loops. While this is more of a design flaw than an intentional attack vector, it opens the door to denial-of-service conditions. Attackers can exploit recursive routing vulnerabilities to create loops that flood the network with encapsulated packets, consuming bandwidth, CPU resources, and memory on routers and switches. This type of attack can lead to network outages or significant performance degradation, especially in environments where network devices are already operating near capacity. Proper route filtering and separation between the tunnel's transport path and its encapsulated destinations are essential to prevent this scenario.

GRE tunnels also present challenges in terms of firewall and intrusion detection or prevention system visibility. Many security appliances are not GRE-aware, which means that they treat GRE packets as opaque or unknown. Because the payload is encapsulated within a GRE header, traditional security tools may be unable to inspect the inner contents unless they perform explicit GRE decapsulation. This allows malicious payloads or unauthorized data to bypass standard inspection mechanisms. In effect, GRE can become a blind spot in the network, enabling attackers to hide traffic from network monitoring systems, intrusion detection tools, or data loss prevention mechanisms. Even sophisticated firewalls may be unable to enforce application-layer security controls on GRE traffic unless specifically configured to recognize and analyze GRE payloads.

GRE tunnels can also be abused for data exfiltration. If an attacker gains access to a device within a trusted network and is able to initiate GRE sessions to an external host, they can encapsulate stolen data inside GRE packets and send it out without detection. Since GRE is not commonly used in many enterprise environments, this traffic may be overlooked by security teams or treated as benign background traffic. Furthermore, if outbound firewall rules are not tightly controlled, GRE packets can traverse the edge of the network freely, creating a covert channel for sensitive data to leave the organization. Detecting this type of attack requires deep packet inspection, GRE-aware monitoring, and strict egress filtering policies.

GRE's lack of session tracking also creates vulnerabilities. Because GRE is stateless, tunnel endpoints do not maintain any information about the session beyond basic interface status and reachability. This makes it difficult to detect anomalous behavior such as repeated tunnel resets, asymmetric traffic patterns, or unexpected source IPs. Without session awareness, administrators have limited tools to monitor or control how the tunnel is used. Attackers can exploit this by launching intermittent attacks or hiding their traffic within legitimate GRE flows, reducing the chances of detection and increasing the difficulty of forensic analysis after an incident.

GRE tunnels that traverse devices performing Network Address Translation (NAT) are particularly prone to issues if not properly configured. Many NAT devices do not natively support GRE protocol 47, and when they do, tracking sessions accurately is often unreliable due to the lack of port information. This can result in dropped packets, tunnel instability, or inadvertent exposure of internal IP addresses. Attackers aware of NAT traversal weaknesses may exploit these inconsistencies to disrupt tunnel operations or map internal network structures by sending crafted GRE packets and analyzing responses.

A less obvious but equally critical risk arises from configuration drift and lack of audit controls. In large environments with numerous GRE tunnels, configurations can become inconsistent over time, leading to unintentional exposure or misrouting of traffic. When GRE tunnels are deployed without centralized oversight, unauthorized endpoints may be added, credentials may not be rotated, or outdated encryption policies may persist. If security teams do not have visibility into GRE tunnel configurations and their operational status, risk accumulates silently until a breach or service interruption occurs. Strong change control processes, configuration management systems, and regular tunnel audits are essential for mitigating these hidden threats.

To secure GRE tunnels against these risks, organizations must adopt a layered security strategy. This includes encrypting GRE payloads with IPsec, implementing firewall rules that restrict GRE traffic to known source and destination pairs, and using GRE key fields to separate and identify different logical tunnels. Tunnel endpoints should be hardened, monitored continuously, and integrated with logging systems that track tunnel creation, status changes, and anomalies. Security teams must ensure that intrusion detection systems are capable of parsing GRE encapsulated traffic or that decapsulation occurs at a choke point where inspection tools are deployed. Strict egress filtering, session timeouts, and anomaly detection help prevent abuse and support rapid incident response.

Ultimately, while GRE serves as a powerful and efficient tunneling mechanism, its use must be governed by a comprehensive security framework. The very characteristics that make GRE flexible and lightweight also expose it to a wide range of security threats. Without appropriate safeguards, GRE can become a conduit for data leaks, unauthorized access, and infrastructure attacks. By understanding these risks and integrating GRE into broader network security policies and practices, organizations can safely leverage its capabilities while maintaining the confidentiality, integrity, and availability of their networks and data.

Future of GRE Tunneling

Generic Routing Encapsulation, commonly known as GRE, has long been a cornerstone of IP tunneling in enterprise and service provider networks. Originally designed as a simple method to encapsulate one protocol within another, GRE has stood the test of time due to its flexibility, low overhead, and protocol independence. As networks have evolved from simple point-to-point structures to highly dynamic, distributed, and virtualized environments, the utility of GRE has remained consistent. Yet the question arises whether GRE will maintain its relevance in the rapidly changing networking landscape dominated by cloud-native applications, zero trust architectures, software-defined networks, and increasing demands for security and performance. While newer technologies like VXLAN, Geneve, and SRv6 offer advanced capabilities, the future of GRE tunneling appears to be shaped not by obsolescence, but by adaptation and integration into broader network strategies.

One of the strongest indicators of GRE's continued presence in modern networks is its integration with existing and emerging technologies rather than its replacement. GRE's simplicity is its strength. It continues to serve as the underlying transport mechanism for various overlay protocols and is commonly used in combination with IPsec to build encrypted VPNs. In hybrid cloud scenarios, GRE tunnels offer a quick and efficient method to connect on-premises data centers to cloud environments, especially in cases where native cloud VPN solutions fall short in supporting dynamic routing or multicast traffic. This kind of adaptability ensures that GRE remains a relevant option for organizations transitioning to cloud-first or multi-cloud architectures.

GRE's role in software-defined networking is another area where its future is being redefined. While SDN often abstracts the underlying transport mechanisms, the reality is that GRE tunnels continue to play a role in facilitating connectivity between SDN domains, especially when interoperability is required across heterogeneous platforms. Network engineers can establish GRE tunnels between SDN controllers, between SD-WAN edge devices, or across legacy infrastructure to maintain compatibility and extend the capabilities of modern control planes. In this context, GRE becomes a foundational component in hybrid networking solutions, linking traditional and programmable environments in a seamless, policy-driven fashion.

The future of GRE is also closely tied to the growing demand for service chaining and traffic engineering. As more services are virtualized and delivered via network functions virtualization platforms, the need to steer traffic through a series of service nodes without impacting the original IP header becomes more important. GRE's ability to encapsulate traffic with minimal transformation makes it suitable for these environments. When combined with technologies such as VRF, policy-based routing, and quality of service mechanisms, GRE enables precise control over how traffic is forwarded through firewalls, load balancers, and intrusion detection systems. This utility is expected to become even more valuable as networks continue to emphasize microsegmentation and fine-grained traffic control.

Security remains a central concern in the future development of any tunneling technology, and GRE is no exception. While GRE on its own lacks encryption and authentication features, its use alongside security protocols like IPsec provides a secure framework suitable for many enterprise deployments. Looking forward, it is expected that GRE implementations will increasingly integrate more tightly with native security capabilities. Vendors may offer enhanced GRE modules that support inline authentication, tagging, or telemetry features to assist with security enforcement, auditing, and visibility. Such enhancements would align GRE with the needs of zero trust networking, where every packet is subject to inspection and policy verification regardless of its origin.

Another emerging area for GRE lies in its compatibility with IPv6 transition mechanisms. As organizations move toward full IPv6 adoption, GRE continues to serve as a bridging tool for encapsulating IPv6 traffic across legacy IPv4 networks and vice versa. This transitional use case will persist for many years in environments where upgrading every component of the network to support dual-stack or native IPv6 is not yet feasible. GRE's lightweight architecture and broad support make it an ideal candidate for these transitional deployments, ensuring that connectivity is preserved while broader modernization efforts continue.

Performance optimization is also poised to redefine the use of GRE in the future. Traditional GRE processing is often handled in software, which limits its scalability in high-performance environments. However, advancements in hardware offloading and network interface card capabilities now allow GRE encapsulation and decapsulation to be performed at line rate. This dramatically reduces the CPU overhead associated with GRE tunnels and opens the door for GRE to be used in environments that demand low-latency and high-throughput performance, such as real-time media delivery, high-frequency trading, and cloud-scale applications. As hardware support becomes more widespread, GRE will be increasingly viable in performance-sensitive scenarios.

Automation and orchestration frameworks are another factor influencing GRE's trajectory. As networks grow in complexity and scale, manual configuration of GRE tunnels becomes impractical. The future will see GRE more deeply integrated into network automation tools, enabling dynamic tunnel creation, monitoring, and teardown in response to policy changes, traffic demands, or failure conditions. This integration is particularly beneficial in containerized and microservices environments where connectivity must be established dynamically between workloads that are ephemeral in nature. GRE's stateless design and ease of implementation make it well-suited to this level of agility and programmability.

The rise of edge computing also introduces new use cases for GRE. With workloads and services being pushed to the edge of the network, GRE can be used to establish lightweight, secure links between edge devices and central data centers. This provides a mechanism for maintaining consistent routing and policy enforcement without the overhead of more complex tunneling protocols. In addition, GRE's ability to encapsulate multicast traffic makes it useful in edge scenarios that involve video distribution, IoT telemetry, or collaborative applications requiring real-time synchronization between nodes.

In global networks where latency and compliance dictate traffic flow decisions, GRE offers a way to control and segment routing paths geographically. Organizations can use GRE tunnels to enforce data locality by directing specific traffic flows through predefined paths, ensuring that sensitive data does not leave designated jurisdictions.

This capability is becoming increasingly relevant in light of regulatory requirements such as GDPR, HIPAA, and data residency laws that demand precise control over data transmission routes.

Despite the emergence of newer tunneling protocols with more sophisticated feature sets, the future of GRE tunneling remains promising due to its foundational role in many network architectures, its ease of deployment, and its compatibility with modern technologies. GRE continues to evolve, not by attempting to replace more advanced tunneling mechanisms, but by complementing them and filling roles where simplicity, versatility, and integration are more important than feature depth. Its continued refinement through hardware acceleration, security enhancements, and orchestration integration will ensure its place in the network engineer's toolkit for years to come, especially in environments where flexibility, interoperability, and control are paramount.

Case Studies in GRE Deployment

The deployment of Generic Routing Encapsulation, or GRE, across a range of industries and network architectures illustrates the protocol's adaptability and resilience. GRE has been successfully implemented in various scenarios, from enabling secure site-to-site connectivity in large multinational enterprises to supporting dynamic routing and segmentation in service provider backbones. These case studies highlight not only the technical aspects of GRE configuration but also the strategic decisions that drive its selection as a tunneling mechanism. By examining real-world applications of GRE, it becomes evident how network engineers leverage its simplicity and flexibility to solve complex connectivity challenges, integrate disparate systems, and enable robust network overlays in both traditional and cloud-centric environments.

In one of the most illustrative examples, a global financial institution with offices in over thirty countries implemented GRE tunnels to interconnect its regional data centers with branch locations. The company faced a challenge with its MPLS provider, which did not support multicast routing across its backbone. Since the institution relied heavily on multicast to distribute financial market data in real time, it needed a solution to transport multicast traffic across the MPLS network without changing the core architecture. GRE tunnels were deployed between branch routers and regional data centers, encapsulating multicast packets and allowing them to traverse the MPLS backbone as unicast GRE packets. The GRE configuration was layered over OSPF to maintain dynamic routing, and GRE-over-IPsec was used to ensure encryption and compliance with strict financial data protection policies. The deployment succeeded in preserving application functionality without requiring changes to the service provider's infrastructure, demonstrating GRE's value in creating overlay networks that solve limitations in underlying transport.

Another compelling use case involved a large healthcare organization that utilized GRE tunnels to securely integrate its newly acquired clinics into its existing IT infrastructure. The challenge was that each clinic operated an independent network and used varying firewall and routing configurations. Rather than overhaul each site's configuration, the healthcare provider deployed GRE tunnels from the corporate data center to the edge devices at each clinic. These tunnels encapsulated IPv6 traffic within IPv4 packets, allowing the central network to deliver modernized IPv6 services across an existing IPv4-only WAN. Dynamic routing protocols were run across the tunnels to automate route distribution, while strict access control policies were enforced at the tunnel endpoints. This approach enabled the healthcare provider to centralize services such as electronic health record systems and secure remote desktop access without interrupting clinical operations. In an industry where downtime and data breaches can have life-threatening consequences, GRE provided the necessary transport flexibility and operational stability to achieve rapid integration.

A telecommunications service provider in South America used GRE tunnels to extend Layer 3 VPN services to remote rural areas that lacked MPLS connectivity. The provider deployed GRE tunnels over broadband internet links, using them as transport paths between remote customer premises equipment and centralized route reflectors. Each GRE tunnel was mapped to a specific virtual routing and forwarding (VRF) instance, allowing traffic segregation between different customers. The GRE keys and tunnel source addresses were assigned uniquely for each customer to prevent cross-routing. Routing control was managed with BGP, and QoS policies were applied to GRE tunnel interfaces to prioritize voice and video services. This configuration enabled the provider to deliver business-grade connectivity services to rural customers at a fraction of the cost of laying dedicated circuits, proving that GRE tunnels can serve as a scalable and cost-effective alternative to more complex VPN solutions.

In the education sector, a university system with multiple campuses used GRE tunnels to create a unified research network over the public internet. Researchers required access to high-performance computing clusters, shared storage, and collaboration platforms hosted at the flagship campus. The university's central IT department established GRE tunnels between each campus's border routers, enabling seamless communication across geographically dispersed sites. The GRE tunnels encapsulated all Layer 3 traffic and carried OSPF routes, ensuring that researchers experienced the same network behavior regardless of location. Traffic shaping and monitoring were performed at the GRE interfaces, allowing network administrators to enforce fair usage policies and ensure optimal performance for latency-sensitive applications. This use of GRE enhanced academic collaboration and reduced dependence on commercial VPN providers, lowering costs while improving connectivity and control.

In another scenario, a logistics company operating across multiple continents used nested GRE tunnels to support a multi-layered network design. The company needed to segment logistics, administrative, and customer service networks while maintaining centralized routing control. The inner GRE tunnels were used to isolate traffic between business units, and each inner tunnel was encapsulated within an outer GRE tunnel that provided global transport connectivity over the internet. This nesting allowed the company to enforce security policies at both the segment and transport levels, while also enabling centralized logging and monitoring of all encapsulated traffic. The design allowed for rapid onboarding of new warehouses and distribution centers by replicating a predefined GRE template. Site engineers needed only to establish connectivity to the outer GRE endpoint, and all routing, segmentation, and security policies would be automatically applied through automation scripts. This approach demonstrated how GRE's layering capabilities could be used to build sophisticated and scalable network architectures tailored to dynamic business needs.

A defense contractor utilized GRE tunnels to interconnect secure enclaves across international locations while maintaining strict compartmentalization. Due to the sensitivity of the data being transmitted, GRE was deployed over IPsec with mandatory endpoint authentication and FIPS-compliant encryption. GRE tunnels allowed routing between enclave gateways while preventing direct access between internal systems. Dynamic routing protocols were tightly scoped, and traffic was filtered at the tunnel interfaces using extended access control lists and route maps. The design allowed for real-time coordination between geographically distributed teams while meeting the rigorous security standards imposed by military and governmental oversight bodies. GRE's compatibility with legacy systems, as well as its support for carrying non-IP protocols, was instrumental in maintaining interoperability with various tactical and operational systems used by field personnel.

These case studies demonstrate that GRE's strengths lie in its adaptability to diverse network requirements, its simplicity of deployment, and its ability to function as a foundational transport layer for more complex services. Whether addressing limitations in legacy infrastructure, enabling rapid expansion, facilitating compliance, or supporting service differentiation, GRE provides a practical solution that bridges gaps in modern network design. The flexibility to encapsulate any Layer 3 protocol, the compatibility with routing protocols, and the support for integration with security mechanisms allow GRE to continue serving as a critical tool for network architects across industries and geographies. Through thoughtful design and strategic application, GRE remains not just a legacy tunneling protocol but a relevant and powerful mechanism in the evolving landscape of enterprise and service provider networking.

Building Scalable VPNs with GRE

Generic Routing Encapsulation, or GRE, has become a fundamental building block in the construction of scalable virtual private networks across a variety of network architectures. As organizations expand across geographical regions, integrate multiple data centers, and transition to hybrid cloud environments, the need for flexible, reliable, and easily deployable VPN solutions becomes critical. GRE offers a protocol-agnostic tunneling mechanism that allows encapsulation of any Layer 3 protocol over IP networks, which makes it an attractive option for enterprises and service providers aiming to extend private connectivity over public or shared infrastructure. The scalability of VPNs built with GRE lies in the protocol's simplicity, its broad compatibility with routing protocols, and its ability to be layered with other technologies to provide encryption, segmentation, and traffic engineering.

A scalable VPN must support the growing number of remote offices, data centers, cloud regions, and mobile users that require secure access to central resources. GRE supports this model by creating point-to-point tunnels between routers or firewall devices, forming a virtual overlay that connects disparate parts of the network into a cohesive whole. The process of establishing GRE tunnels is straightforward: a source and destination IP address is configured on each endpoint, and the tunnel interface is brought up using a unique tunnel ID or key if desired. This simplicity allows network engineers to deploy GRE tunnels rapidly and with minimal configuration overhead. As the network grows, additional tunnels can be spun up using the same configuration model, ensuring consistency and reducing deployment time.

One of the key advantages GRE offers in building scalable VPNs is its ability to work seamlessly with dynamic routing protocols. When multiple GRE tunnels are deployed across a large network, protocols such as OSPF, EIGRP, or BGP can run over the GRE interfaces to automatically exchange route information. This dynamic exchange eliminates the need for static routing in large-scale deployments and enables automatic failover, route redistribution, and policy enforcement. In hub-and-spoke designs, where many branch offices connect to a central data center, GRE tunnels can be used to create spoke-to-hub links, and routing protocols ensure that all branches can reach each other through the central hub without requiring full-mesh tunnel configuration. For organizations needing full-mesh connectivity, GRE tunnels combined with route reflectors or route summarization techniques can manage routing table sizes while supporting direct branch-to-branch communication.

Security is a critical requirement in any VPN solution, and while GRE does not provide encryption or authentication by itself, it integrates smoothly with IPsec to provide a secure overlay. GRE-over-IPsec combines the flexibility of GRE with the strong security guarantees of IPsec. The GRE tunnel encapsulates the original packet, and the IPsec layer encrypts and authenticates the entire GRE payload. This configuration allows the use of dynamic routing protocols, multicast traffic, and non-IP protocols across secure connections, something that native IPsec tunnels cannot easily support. For scalable VPN architectures, GRE-over-IPsec ensures that even as new tunnels are added and routing becomes more complex, security is maintained without sacrificing functionality.

GRE also supports segmentation and multi-tenancy in scalable VPN environments. By using tunnel keys and binding GRE tunnels to different virtual routing and forwarding (VRF) instances, network operators can logically separate traffic from different departments, customers, or services. This model is particularly effective in managed service environments, where a service provider offers VPN connectivity to multiple customers over a shared infrastructure. Each customer receives a set of GRE tunnels bound to their own VRF, ensuring complete isolation of routing and data while sharing the same physical underlay. As new customers are onboarded, additional GRE tunnels can be provisioned within minutes using templated configurations and automation tools.

Automation plays a vital role in scaling GRE-based VPNs efficiently. Tools like Ansible, Python scripts, and vendor-specific orchestration platforms can automate the creation, monitoring, and teardown of GRE tunnels. These tools ensure that configurations are applied consistently across devices, reducing human error and speeding up deployment timelines. In dynamic environments such as cloud-based workloads or SD-WAN edge networks, automation allows tunnels to be established on-demand, following predefined policies based on workload requirements, geographic location, or performance thresholds. By integrating GRE tunnel management into the broader orchestration framework, organizations achieve the agility needed to scale rapidly without compromising operational integrity.

Performance optimization is another factor in building scalable VPNs with GRE. As the number of tunnels increases and traffic volumes grow, it becomes essential to manage bandwidth, latency, and packet loss across the network. GRE interfaces can be configured with quality of service (QoS) settings to prioritize traffic types such as voice, video, or real-time data. Tunnel traffic can be monitored for performance metrics using IP SLA or telemetry tools, enabling proactive management of congestion and early detection of degradation. In high-throughput environments, GRE offloading to hardware or using routers with specialized network processing units can significantly enhance performance and reduce CPU load, ensuring that scalability does not come at the cost of efficiency.

GRE tunnels are also useful for supporting failover and redundancy in scalable VPN architectures. Multiple GRE tunnels can be established between sites using diverse paths or ISPs. Routing protocols can select the best path based on cost or policy, and failover mechanisms such as GRE keepalives or BFD can detect tunnel outages and switch traffic to backup tunnels automatically. This level of resilience is critical for organizations with zero-downtime requirements, as it ensures that communication remains intact even in the face of infrastructure failure or provider outages. In addition, load balancing can be implemented using equal-cost multipath routing (ECMP) across GRE tunnels, distributing traffic evenly and maximizing available bandwidth.

As organizations adopt multi-cloud strategies and distribute applications across hybrid environments, GRE provides a consistent and vendor-neutral method for connecting resources. GRE tunnels can be established between on-premises routers and cloud gateways, between multiple cloud regions, or between workloads running in virtualized environments. This flexibility ensures that no matter where workloads are deployed, they can communicate securely and efficiently using a standardized tunneling protocol. As cloud providers continue to support GRE natively or through virtual appliances, the use of GRE for cloud VPNs is expected to grow, offering a reliable option for extending corporate networks into cloud ecosystems.

GRE's adaptability, ease of deployment, and broad protocol support make it an ideal foundation for scalable VPN design. Whether used as a standalone tunneling method or in conjunction with IPsec, dynamic routing, QoS, and automation, GRE enables networks to grow organically while maintaining control, performance, and security. Its continued relevance in modern architectures ensures that organizations of all sizes can build scalable, flexible, and resilient VPN infrastructures capable of meeting the demands of distributed and dynamic digital operations.

GRE Tunneling in Real-Time Applications

Generic Routing Encapsulation, or GRE, is a widely used tunneling protocol designed to encapsulate a variety of Layer 3 protocols over IP networks. While GRE is often celebrated for its flexibility and simplicity, its application in real-time communication systems presents unique challenges and opportunities. Real-time applications such as voice over IP, video conferencing, telemedicine, financial trading, and collaborative platforms depend on low latency, minimal jitter, and high availability to function correctly. In these environments, every millisecond counts, and the introduction of any additional layer of encapsulation, such as that added by GRE, must be carefully managed to preserve the performance expectations of time-sensitive services.

The most compelling reason to use GRE in real-time application deployments is its ability to create consistent and predictable network overlays across heterogeneous infrastructure. Many real-time services are deployed across hybrid or distributed architectures, where some endpoints reside in cloud environments, others in on-premises data centers, and still others in edge computing nodes. GRE facilitates a uniform transport mechanism, allowing these disparate systems to interconnect over existing IP infrastructure without the need for native multicast support or protocol compatibility across all intermediate hops. In real-time video broadcasting, for example, GRE tunnels can be used to encapsulate multicast streams and deliver them across networks that do not support multicast routing natively. This guarantees that high-volume video traffic reaches all intended endpoints without relying on specialized underlay capabilities.

However, the introduction of GRE encapsulation adds additional header overhead to each packet, typically around 24 bytes. This overhead increases the total size of the packet and can result in fragmentation if the encapsulated packet exceeds the maximum transmission unit of the path. Fragmentation is particularly problematic in real-time applications because it increases processing delays and the risk of packet loss. To address this, network administrators must carefully configure tunnel MTU settings and enable path MTU discovery mechanisms to ensure packets are transmitted without fragmentation. TCP MSS clamping may also be implemented at the tunnel interface to ensure that transport layer protocols do not exceed safe packet sizes. In addition, real-time applications that use UDP rather than TCP are often more vulnerable to the effects of packet loss and jitter, so maintaining a reliable and low-latency path through the GRE tunnel is essential.

Another challenge of using GRE in real-time applications is the stateless nature of the protocol. GRE does not include any inherent mechanism for congestion control, packet ordering, or delivery guarantees. It simply encapsulates and forwards packets. As such, real-time applications relying on GRE must depend on the underlying transport network for quality of service and must use additional protocols or external monitoring tools to assess the health and performance of the tunnel. GRE interfaces can be integrated with quality of service policies at the router level, allowing prioritized treatment of voice and video traffic within the tunnel. Class-based queuing, traffic shaping, and policing can all be applied to GRE tunnel interfaces, ensuring that real-time packets are not delayed behind bulk data transfers or less time-sensitive services. This approach is essential for maintaining low jitter and consistent throughput, especially during peak traffic conditions.

To further support real-time applications, GRE can be combined with Bidirectional Forwarding Detection (BFD) or GRE keepalives to monitor tunnel health and detect failures quickly. If a GRE tunnel becomes unstable or fails, these mechanisms allow for rapid convergence of routing protocols and failover to backup paths. In mission-critical real-time environments, such as emergency services communication or remote surgical operations, the ability to detect and recover from tunnel failure within milliseconds is non-negotiable. BFD running over GRE tunnels ensures that link health is continuously monitored, allowing routing decisions to adapt dynamically to maintain uninterrupted service. In multi-tunnel configurations, dynamic routing protocols like OSPF or BGP can be used to distribute real-time traffic across available GRE tunnels based on policy, load, or latency, adding resilience and scalability to the network design.

One important advantage GRE offers in real-time application deployment is its compatibility with encryption protocols like IPsec. Real-time traffic is often sensitive and subject to strict regulatory requirements, particularly in sectors like healthcare, finance, and defense. GRE-over-IPsec enables the secure transmission of real-time data across public networks, combining GRE's flexibility with the confidentiality and integrity provided by encryption. This configuration allows organizations to extend their secure communication environments beyond the boundaries of their physical infrastructure without sacrificing the routing and protocol compatibility necessary for complex real-time workflows. When implemented correctly, GRE-over-IPsec tunnels provide both the transport abstraction and the security assurances required to support sensitive, high-priority communications.

Real-time applications are increasingly deployed in containerized or virtualized environments, especially in edge computing and multi-cloud ecosystems. GRE's simplicity makes it an attractive tunneling method in such scenarios, where agility and programmability are key. Automation tools and orchestration platforms can be used to create, modify, and remove GRE tunnels dynamically as workloads are instantiated or migrated. This ensures that real-time services maintain consistent connectivity regardless of where they are deployed. In edge deployments, for instance, GRE tunnels can link local processing nodes to centralized control centers, enabling real-time analytics, monitoring, or command and control operations. These tunnels can be provisioned on demand in response to device registration, application events, or network policy triggers, allowing for seamless scale-up and scale-down operations in highly dynamic environments.

Monitoring and visibility are critical to maintaining the performance of real-time applications over GRE tunnels. Standard monitoring tools may not have insight into the encapsulated payload, especially when tunnels traverse multiple network segments. As such, it is essential to deploy GRE-aware performance monitoring and telemetry solutions. These tools can analyze traffic entering and exiting GRE tunnels, measuring latency, jitter, packet loss, and throughput in real time. Network engineers can use this data to identify bottlenecks, fine-tune QoS policies, or trigger automated responses when performance thresholds are breached. For example, a drop in voice call quality or an increase in video buffering could indicate tunnel congestion or misconfiguration, which can be addressed through real-time alerts or policy adjustments.

Despite the challenges, GRE remains a valuable tool in supporting real-time communication systems due to its protocol agnosticism, wide support across network devices, and ease of integration. While other tunneling protocols like VXLAN or LISP may offer more advanced features for specific use cases, GRE's simplicity and extensibility make it well suited to environments where deterministic behavior and rapid deployment are essential. Organizations leveraging GRE for real-time applications must design their networks with careful attention to MTU settings, QoS configuration, tunnel health monitoring, and failover strategy. When these factors are addressed, GRE becomes a reliable transport for time-sensitive traffic, supporting the growing demand for real-time connectivity in a digital world that depends on instant communication, high-speed interaction, and uninterrupted service delivery across increasingly complex infrastructures.